NORFOLK'S WAR

NORFOLK'S WAR

Frank Meeres

AMBERLEY

First published 2016

Amberley Publishing
The Hill, Stroud
Gloucestershire, GL5 4EP

www. amberley-books.com

Copyright © Frank Meeres, 2016

British Library Cataloguing in Publication Data. A catalogue record for this book is available from the
British Library.

ISBN 978 1 4456 2092 3 (print)
ISBN 978 1 4456 2102 9 (ebook)

Origination by Amberley Publishing.
Printed in the UK.

CONTENTS

INTRODUCTION

Norfolk's men, women and children all played their part in Britain's first total war. Almost every village has its memorial giving honour to the dead. The First World War saw the start of many aspects of war that were to be repeated a generation later – conscription, rationing, digging for victory, air raids and blackouts. Many people hoped that it would be 'the war to end all wars' but a century of wars has shattered this hope. Despite this, the years have allowed us to increase our appreciation of the courage of our ancestors, ordinary Norfolk people caught up in horrific times.

Heroes and heroines all.

The nurses of Ward 6, Norfolk War Hospital.
(ACC 2009/103)

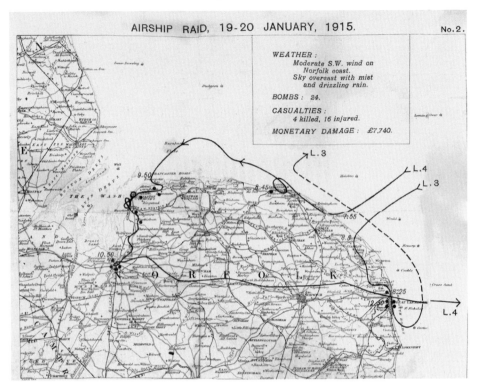

Britain's first fatal air raid. (MC 2321/1)

1

THE CHILDREN

The First World War is often called the first *total war* – everyone was involved, including children. Boys in the relatively new organisation of the Boy Scouts played vital roles in a coastal county like Norfolk, as diaries and reports made plain. On 8 August 1914, just four days after war was declared, Ingham scouts received a telegram from Colonel Charles, the county commissioner, that the Admiralty required eight scouts to assist coastguards at Palling. A later report to the Scout association says that the Scouts remained on duty for three weeks, and 'gave complete satisfaction to the Coastguard Officer'. The Scoutmaster's diary gives more details of the events:

Telegram was acted on immediately. Was unable to raise more than one boy – G Whittleton from Ingham troop, but sent in three Palling boys and the rest from Stalham, with Divers as Scoutmaster. Camped them on piece of ground by Sandhills hired by Atkins for Scouts but received strong protest from an ass called Watson, Director of Kew, who resides just there. Said, as his wife expected a baby by the end of the month, couldn't have them there. Expostulated with him and left them there. Wife is militant suffragette. On calling out of boys for Telegraph work had to take off Divers and one tent and left boys under Roy Spanton, till 17th when I first and then Scoutmasters in rotation took duty with them. Boys had got on pretty well alone, but had got slack in detail of keeping Camp ship-shape. On that day we shifted camp to be out of bad influence of Watson and pitched another tent for Scoutmaster.

During first day or two boys saw much in way of activity at sea, and aeroplanes, but have not been of any very serious assistance to Coastguard.

The 'telegraph work' mentioned was rather less successful. According to the report later presented to the Association,

The day after the instalment of the Patrol further Orders were received to send out Scouts to guard telegraph cable lines between North Walsham and Scottow. The orders were received at 8 pm on Sunday Aug 9 and a large part of the section of line was patrolled by noon next day while the whole section was taken up during the afternoon … The boys kept watch for four days, night and day, and did their duty remarkably well. Great credit is due to boys, parents, employers and Scoutmasters for the smooth way in which this unexpected mobilisation was carried out.

However, as the Scoutmaster's diary makes plain, there was a good deal of chaos left unmentioned in this report. On 9 August, Ingham scout troop received a copy of a telegram sent by the Government to Colonel Charles calling on scouts to watch trunk cable lines to prevent them being tapped or cut. The troop swung into action:

At once sent for Cordwell and warned Scouts their services might be wanted, and went off to see Col Charles. On return consulted with Cordwell and Stebbings and issued for their troop slips of paper to be handed to each boy with this order: *To Scout X. Your services are required by the Government for duty beginning today. Report yourself to me at [left blank] in uniform with Great Coat and complete camp kit. I shilling a day.*

Our boys were ordered to report here at 11 am on Monday. At 6 am JG started to North Walsham to make enquiries about the Cable line and after much difficulty found that it ran, not via Tunstead as advised by Col Charles but via Worstead and Scottow. I went at same time to Honing and Worstead and whipped up Scouts there. At about 11.15 we got off with 6 Palling Scouts and camp outfit, and by noon we had placed all our boys along a line from North Walsham main road to Cook's farm at Worstead. Pitched camp in Sandpit close by. Cordwell, with Catfield, Ludham and some Hickling boys turned up soon after us and got on line from nearly into North Walsham to our end. Worstead, Honing and Stalham boys came on duty about 3 pm and divided between them the road from Cook's farm nearly to Scottow. Worstead boys on duty lived in their homes, we had four camps – Catfield & Ludham; Ingham & Palling: Honing; Stalham – the latter in a barn.

There were a total of sixty-seven boys involved, with nine scoutmasters or helpers. Each group was given a 'beat':

The Ingham beat was divided into three sections each of which had a book carried by the boy or boys on watch, for notes. Night watches were taken by boys in pairs, except one or two over seventeen who went alone, and were for 2 hours the first night, and three hours subsequently. Each boy, except some very small ones, did one watch at night.

Found road patrolled once in day and once at night by a G.P.O. man on a bicycle. The day man reported on Aug 10 that wire had been cut at Cromer and tapped at Bacton during the night. Said that the wires here form a 'Cable park' going via Bacton to London, but that the Cable was now cut at sea deliberately and the wires used for inland military purposes and not for telegraph but for telephones.

All boys did work well except two small ones, Wright and Ellis, who got homesick and cried, and were sent back on Aug 12. They were not overworked, only silly. On same day Col. Charles came over, rather despondent about whole thing. All other troops had failed to take correct positions and much shifting had to be done. The Wroxham troop which should have taken on at our end failed to get into touch until Thursday 13th. Part of the time they watched a road without wires at all.

During this day [12 Aug] we found North Walsham ordered to cover our own ground (they had only about 8 boys to do it too!) while subsequently Wroxham boys were ordered over the whole of the road covered by the Stalham troop!

As a result I had a conference of our Scoutmasters and Rev Nash of North Walsham on Thursday 13th, 10 am. We then decided to send off all boys under 14, as government refused to pay for them, and we re-arranged our beats to take in North Walsham.

Scouts under 14 were sent back, Stalham ones at once, Ingham and Palling on Friday 14th, walking. On the Thursday I received notice that no night duty was required, so thinking the whole thing was a farce I went over on Friday to see Col. Charles and offer to take off Scouts and get the day job done by Cyclist volunteers. On arrival I found that orders were received to withdraw all the Scouts at once, pay ceasing on 4th day!

Naturally it was most difficult to do, but we managed by means of two journeys with both cars to get the whole thing broken up the same afternoon. Fortunately our own tents were already packed to be erected at Worstead Vicarage.

The Scouts made themselves useful in many other ways as well, selling stamps to raise money for War Relief (one boy was especially praised for selling 108 of them), and doing volunteer work at Ingham Red Cross Hospital.

Even scouts from Norwich were called upon for coast watching. Scoutmaster Charles Bower described the work of the 1st Norwich group at Mundesley in the *Headquarters Gazette*:

On December 23rd [1914] seven boys from the Troop and myself went to Mundesley, Norfolk, for coastguard duty. Mundesley is rather unique for this duty, I think. We were attached to Bacton Coastguard Station, four and a half miles away. Yet we lived at Mundesley, and our duty lay on the highest portion of the cliff, three-quarters of a mile from Mundesley. We were lucky in obtaining an empty cottage to live in, and this the boys kept like the deck of a man-o'-war all the time, scrubbing the floors once a week, and thoroughly brushing and cleaning the place out once a day. We had to keep watch at a tiny shepherd's hut on wheels some feet above the sea and right on the edge of the cliff. The hut was about 6 feet by four feet, and was awfully cold and draughty on a windy night. It was only shower-proof, and any heavy rain, such as we had most of the time we were there, came through.

The boys worked in pairs, four hours on and eight hours off, night and day, and during the whole period we were there, namely from December 23 to February 27th, there were always one or two very wide-awake Scouts on duty at that hut. To get to the hut, one had to traverse three-quarters of a mile of cliff path, where there were numerous landslides during the time we were there, for the cliff is very dangerous ...

Our boys were the first Scouts on the coast to see and report the Zeppelins which dropped bombs on Sheringham, Yarmouth, and Lynn, and Bacton station was the first to report their presence. They were seen there at the same time my boys saw them, and the boys passed the message down there at once.

Scouts on sea watch at
Mundesley. (SO 36/7)

Naturally, Scoutmasters like Bower were very keen to take up arms themselves. By
April 1916, he was in the frontline, writing back a letter with explicit details of the
conditions:

I have had no opportunity of writing while in the trenches as I was on duty day and night and
every minute I had off I fell asleep at once automatically ... We have been shifted again, this
time to an exceedingly hot part of the line. I managed to get my platoon out all right, free from
harm, and am considered very lucky to have got through without any casualties. Of course it
was a stroke of luck pure and simple but I am very thankful for it.

I have lost one of my brother officers, I'm sorry to say, a topping chap, but he is only badly
wounded and not severely, thank goodness. He's in England now, lucky dog! The 'strafe' goes
on here unceasingly day and night with every kind of hellishness known. I had 3 hrs lie down in
72 hrs and so was pretty done up. But now I'm quite fit ...

I have been twice out on patrol in 'No Man's Land' between the English and German lines,
where the dead lie thick on the ground rotting! Pretty awful smell and gruesome, but a very
exciting experience creeping over the parapet with machine guns rattling away at you only a
few yards away.

The two lines are awfully close together here. We didn't feel fear tho', but only awe. Not nice
putting your hand in the dark on a Corpse, is it? Esp. one that's been rotting for six months! I
crept out to inspect the barb wire and repair it with my Orderly, and an old 1st Class Scout in
the platoon behind me. I had to go out twice that night. It was awful the 2nd time, much worse
than the 1st. I was on the job from 12.30–2.30 am, and then on duty as Officer of the Watch
from 3.00 to 6.0 am. I could hear the Germans working plainly, and saw a German Patrol only a
short distance away. It gave me quite a turn I can assure you! They send up brilliant flares every
few minutes. Then you have to be absolutely still, flat on your stomach and you must not make
a sound at all else they can hear you from their trenches. A very undignified position you are
in! You have to crawl all the way, of course very very slowly. The excitement is intense, but it
makes you jolly sleepy after.

Bower suggested that his letter be read to his troop back in Norwich.

Scouts on sea watch at Sea
Palling. (SO 36/7)

Scoutmasters too old to fight could contribute in a great variety of ways. One
keen to help was a man named Bellarby Lowerison from north-west Norfolk. He
made his first contribution in the early days of the war, as this letter shows:

Field Marshal Roberts, 17 September 1914:
Dear Mr Lowerison, I write a line to thank you warmly for your kind response to my appeal for
field glasses. Your glasses will be of the greatest possible service to our Non-Commissioned
Officers in the field. I am asked by the Commanding Officers of Units which are shortly
expected to go to the front to convey their gratitude to the owners of the glasses distributed
among their men.

He had yet more to offer, as demonstrated in a second letter:

Commander Hall, Lowestoft, 29 April 1916:
Scoutmaster Bellerby Lowerison is engaged in Coast Watching service under the Admiralty, which
necessitates his visiting the beach at Heacham and elsewhere at all times of the day or night.

Officer-in-Charge, 3rd Provisional Cyclist Company, Wells, Norfolk, to Private B Lowerison,
8 May 1916:

Sir, The Commanding officer thanks you for your letter of the 5th inst. We have arranged with
Second Lieutenant Pearce at Brancaster that a Pass should be sent you for patrolling the beach in the
neighbourhood of HEACHAM and should be glad if you will co-operate with our men on duty there.

In case of a German raid we should be glad if you will co-operate with our men in the capacity
of Guide in view of your knowledge of the local country. Will you please arrange this with
SERGEANT BODDY the NCO in charge of our men, c/o Mrs Thompson, Westgate, Hunstanton?

The Commanding Officer much appreciates your offer to help our men with regard to
the Miniature Rifle Shooting practice which will be permitted to our men at Hunstanton and
(if arrangements can be made with 2nd Lieutenant Pearce) for the men at Brancaster as well.

Kindly answer the following questions:

(1) Have you a Motor Cycle or push cycle?
(2) What rifle have you got?
(3) What will the cost be for firing on the range?

Girls did not take part in these outdoor activities. They played their part too, but
in more traditional roles, as a report by the Head Girl at Blyth Secondary School,
Norwich, shows:

The object of this Report is to preserve a Record covering the entire period of the war.

FIRST:	£	s.	d.
Belgian Girl Hospitality Fund	70	15	1
Form Money-Boxes Fund	111	11	3
Entertainment Fund and Sales	181	15	4
Miscellaneous Activities	38	2	5
Contributions to Hospital Garments' Material	34	16	8
	437	0	9

The money has been devoted to the following Relief Funds: Lord Mayor's National Relief,
Princess Mary's Soldiers' and Sailors' Christmas, Red Cross, Belgian Relief, Poland and
Galicia, Servian, Red Cross, Star and Garter Building, Camps Library, Edith Cavell Memorial,
Eastern Daily Press plum pudding, King George's for Sailors, Daily Telegraph Naval, Halifax
Disaster, St Dunstan's Hostel for blinded Soldiers and Sailors, To equip a Hut for Sailors from
torpedoed merchant vessels, Christmas gifts for wounded in Norfolk and Norwich Hospital
and Lakenham Hospital, Norwich Hospital Charities, Jenny Lind Infirmary, Norfolk Regiment's
Prisoner of War in Germany, League of Mercy, Voluntary War Work Association, Castle Street
Hospital Supply Depot, Toys for Jenny Lind Xmas Tree.

SECOND:
Form Miscellaneous Activities have been: Egg collection (1,023), magazines for wounded,
sandbags, two prisoners of war in Germany adopted, meat coupons checked for the Local
Food Control Committee.

Nurses in front of a Great Eastern ambulance carriage. (JLD 1/8/1/2)

THIRD:
Needlework Guild. Between 3,000 and 4,000 garments, sewn and knitted, have been made, and distributed as below: The Lady Mayoress' Needlework Guild, Wounded at Norfolk and Norwich Hospital, Jenny Lind Infirmary, Servians, Lady Leicester for the 1st Norfolks, Cambridge Needlework Guild, The Grand Duke Michael for the Sailors, Voluntary War Work Association.

FOURTH:
The School has been responsible for the Swab Department at the Castle Street Hospital Supply Depot, working there on Saturday afternoons from November 1915 to December 1918.

FIFTH:
War Savings Association – Grand Total   £2,693 13 0.

As it became clear that the war was going to last a long time, children in Norfolk schools naturally thought about what their role would be when they came to leave school. The school magazine of Norwich High School for girls ran articles from girls who had recently left and taken up war work, such as this piece by a girl, probably Xenia Muriel, who had left school and gone into munitions.

The defiant farm girl from Ralph
Mottram's *The Spanish Farm*. (MOT 58)

Life in a Munition Factory

Life in a Munition factory is a much more delicate and intricate thing than it appears on the surface.

Yet when you begin, it all seems so simple. You have just to learn your job, do as you are told and that is all.

But later when you have got on a bit, when you have learnt your work and have acquired a certain amount of confidence and above all, when you have realised your responsibilities, then you find that you still have to learn tact and the art of managing other people.

Another thing you have to learn is to mind your own business. You are responsible for a particular bit of the work, but whatever happens you must never interfere with any other.

This sounds obvious, but it is often very difficult to keep to it. If you don't, you invariably manage to jump on somebody's toes.

There are, generally speaking, two classes of women workers.

First there are the operators. They are the people who actually make the war material, whatever it may be. In our factory it is fuse-caps for high explosive shells.

The operators work the machines and in many cases this is pretty hard. The girls vary tremendously in skill, and it is possible to get one to do things which may be beyond the capabilities of another.

There are so many things you have to be careful about too, if you are an operator. For instance, if your machine is not quite clean you may do a great deal of damage. It is possible to fix the fuse in crooked if the machine is choked up with dirt and shavings, and cut a hole aslant when it should be straight.

Then of course the fuse is utterly useless.

Besides the operators, there are also the viewers or gaugers.

They test the work when it comes off the machines, and when they are wrong, they stop the machine and get a 'setter up' to put it right.

If you are a gauger you have to be very much on the spot to stop mistakes directly they occur and to prevent the machines from cutting scrap. You have to work quickly too, if you are gazing at machines to keep pace with the work the operators are putting through.

When the fuse is made, it is washed and lacquered and the most important parts and holes are gauged again.

It is then assembled; the springs, pellets, bolts and screws are put in, the cap is put on – then the fuse is finished.

What you need most of all if you are ever to be any good at munition work is keenness. The person who finds nothing too much trouble, or who is willing to do the same job over again if need be.

Whether keeping guard, knitting garments or raising money, the lives of thousands of Norfolk boys and girls were changed forever as they came face to face with total war.

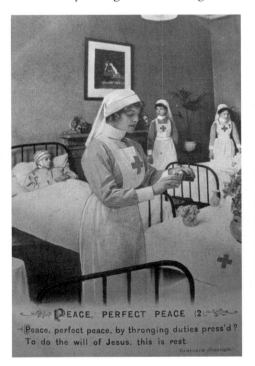

Sentimental cards like these were extremely popular in wartime. (ACC 2013/320)

2

LETTERS FROM A NURSE

Many Norfolk women found their vocation in the traditional female role of nursing. These included women from the upper classes who felt that, as their brothers were going to war, they too should play their part. One such woman was Joyce Carr, one of three daughters of William and Margaret Carr of The Hall, Ditchingham. She was twenty-five in 1915, her sister Dorothy was twenty-three and Alice Katherine (known as 'Kitty') was nineteen. Their brother, William Carr, was serving in the army. This was a very wealthy family, with eight live-in servants at the time of the 1911 census. Their aunt, Mary Carr, lived at Hedenham Hall and in April 1915 she opened this up as a convalescent home. The three sisters appear to have all worked as (unqualified) nurses at Kirstead, a convalescent hospital at Bethel Farm in the village. Joyce went on to serve at the Norwich War Hospital and then at a private hospital run by a cousin in France. Her letters back to her mother give a unique insight into what life was like for young women like Joyce, keen to 'do their bit' for their country in its hour of need.

In 1915, Joyce, then in London, was torn as to what she should do, signing up for six months with Red Cross but then deciding she would rather be a probationer at Thorpe War Hospital in Norwich:

40, Kensington Park Gardens, London, 22 June [1915]:
Thank you, dearest, so much for seeing the Thorpe matron, and writing such a full description of it all. Was it not the greatest mistake that I ever had anything to do with the Red Cross? I am so regretting it now. I showed the Thorpe prospectus about Probationers to my Commandant for though I knew she could not do anything, I thought it would be good for her soul to know how unnecessary the Red Cross is.

I have written this evening to Miss Hamer asking her, if she is taking any Red Cross Special Service nurses, to write to Mrs Furze: and if not suggesting I should come as an ordinary

Exterior views of the
Norfolk War Hospital.
(ACC 2009/103)

probationer (also asking whether in that case I shd. have to sign on for any definite period). Unfortunately, you see, I have already signed and sent in my Red Cross papers, undertaking to nurse for six months when wanted. If Miss Hamer will only have me as an ordinary probationer, I shall ask the Selection Committee to cancel that application. I suppose they will.

So as yet I will buy no uniform, but just get stuff for dresses and send it to Ethel …

PS Most Red X SS nurses seem to be going to Wandsworth, where there is a gigantic hospital for Territorials. I would much rather be at Thorpe.

Two weeks later, she was installed in the Norfolk War Hospital:

NWH, 7 July 1915:

I had a sort of presentiment that I should be the other side of the high road, and so I am. There seems a far more enormous building on this side, which is still being added to, but the tragedy is, that as it is unfinished, there are no patients, so as far as I can see from the other nurses, we spend our time sewing, and there is nothing much to do! Is it not heart-rending to the keen would-be nurse!

I arrived at the same time as another probationer, and we were received by a homely sister named 'Smith', who is the home sister. She took us to tea where [there] were a crowd of nurses all more or less shy and awkward and all talking Norfolk. Then we were brought to our rooms, which are all on both sides of a newly built hut, with corrugated iron sides. They are dear little places, open on the top, so that every sound can be heard, but quite jolly with a wash-stand and chest of drawers, bed and chair. At present I am listening to the young lady next door, talking to the one next door to her, about her clothes and how to arrange them, and the photograph of her 'boy' and where to put it.

After having been shown our rooms we met various little probationers, very wise on a few days standing, and were allowed to go to a concert being held for the soldiers in the main buildings. It was quite jolly. There seemed to be crowds and crowds of them, even now, all in their blue hospital suits. I do hope more will come soon and that this place will fill soon. Surely they would never have got such crowds of probationers as seem to have arrived this week unless they expect wounded soon.

I have now just come back from supper. There were one or two fully fledged nurses there and they were very highty tighty towards the probationers and pleased with themselves because they were on duty in the main buildings. There are four more enormous long huts like this one, that, I suppose, are to be filled with nurses at some time. I have talked to as many of the others as possible. They tell me that we have a great many meals, beginning with breakfast at 7.30. Before that we have to do our rooms and make our beds. Our free hours are from 5 to 8, or till 10 if we get off supper.

I shall be rather grieved if I have to stay here sewing for very long, I must say. It will be different if any men come.

NWH, 13 July 1915:

I had rather a shock coming back the other day to find the gates shut at the bottom of the drive: I thought perhaps I was too late. But as a matter of fact the side door was open and I was in plenty of time … A good many new probationers have come, rather better class than the last I think. There are three or four quite nice girls who have worked some time in the

American Hospital. They seem quite nice, and apparently ladies, but cling together very much and I don't know anyone else … I find that night duty does last for two months, but I am off one day or night each month, when I can come home during the time.

There was a convoy to the Norwich hospital on Saturday, but nothing here. There are only about 280 men here now.

It's funny that French's despatch should be immediately followed by Buchan's descriptive article, but is it not all terrible? I am more and more depressed by wondering when it will end. Why did not we have conscription and some definite organisation ages ago?

NWH, undated:

I have just been told that I have been transferred to the main building, and that I am to go on duty there tomorrow. I am rather sorry, as some nice girls have come here, whom I shall be sorry to leave, but more because of leaving my jolly little room. I may have to share with others over there, very likely, and that might easily be unbearable.

However, I must just do what I am told.

NWH, 17 July 1915:

I am liking it very well in the wards. The work is not at all hard now, as we are so empty. Only 23 men in one ward where there are 50 beds. When I have more time I will describe it more fully. It is most extraordinary untidy and free and easy, far more so than Kirstead even! I was almost shocked.

Ethel Morgan tells me that a charming boy named Nunn has gone from her ward to Aunt Mary's and that Aunt Mary must be kind to him. He has written that he very much approves of the *Tante* [Aunt], but does not like the Sister! … I am still sleeping in the huts.

NWH, 19 July 1915:

I am still sleeping at the huts but will probably have to move soon as I am definitely to work down at the Main Buildings. The Ward that I am in at present, 2B, is a large one upstairs in a detached building. There is one large ward, two smaller ones, three or four single rooms, a dining room, a bathroom a scullery and a pantry in it. The men there at present are very slightly wounded, most of them, and only two are in bed. The others do most of the work, and all the washing up.

There is an orderly, who also does a little, and a charwoman of a morning. Then there is the Sister, a staff nurse, and at present two probationers besides myself (Besides the night staff). So you see we are not desperately busy. But it is such a large place that it takes a good deal of keeping clean, and there are perpetually meals to be prepared or cleared away. It all looks frightfully untidy, as the men spend most of their time lying on their beds, so I am not exactly proud of the appearance of the ward. Also the meals are untidy, with no grace at the end, so that the men leap up and go away at the end.

I do not much like the other probationer, Miss Downing, but the second one, Nurse Madox, an asylum one who has been ill but came back today. Is much more active and stirring and worth three of her.

My work is much what it was in V.A.D. hospitals – sweeping, dusting, cutting bread and butter, and being allowed to take temperatures. I never know beforehand whether I am to have my 3 hours in the morning afternoon or evening. Yesterday it was evening, so I got to church. Today it is afternoon.

It was then suggested to Joyce that she should nurse at a hospital in France run by her cousin, 'Cousin Minnie':

NWH, 8 September 1915, 3.30 a.m.:
Of course I was tremendously excited by your letter yesterday morning, and of course it would be delightful to go and nurse at the Mondeville hospital. But all the same I hesitated, because it seems rather cowardly to run away from this old place, especially if they are going to be busy, just as I am beginning to get more or less useful … I grieve to say there was some fussation here yesterday. Four of the men had passes to go out, and came back drunk. Sister was away and the staff nurse reported them and it is very grievous and the reputation of the ward is gone. Needless to say this is not to be spread abroad at all.

NWH, 14 September 1915:
I have not heard anything about my passport yet. I have been thinking that it will probably [be] impossible to go into the French embassy or whatever it is on Sat afternoon or Sunday. So I shall probably not be able to go till Monday anyhow … We then went to Mousehold. There were no aeroplanes out, but we saw them in their sheds … There are rumours that Zepps are coming again tonight, but we are still allowed lights so far, so they cannot be near anyway.

NWH, 16 September 1915:
Oh I had such difficulty in filling in that passport: I hope you will think it will pass me all right. It really is extraordinarily difficult to describe each feature in an ordinary face. I would have left it to you, only it had to be in my own handwriting. Can you send to fetch me on Friday morning? … If you can't let me know statim and instanter, and I must arrange for a cab.

Havre to Trouville Bateau [boat], 21 September 1915:
I am very pleased with my travels so far. I have found that I can get on to Caen this evening, by steamer as far as Trouville, and then by train, arriving at 8, so I have wired to Cousin Minnie to say that I am coming.

There was a great scrimmage and fussation at Southampton about having our passports examined, and everyone pushed and squeezed. But as soon as I got on the boat all was comfortable. I was given a berth in a cabin with quite a nice other woman who was going on to meet her husband in Paris. The boat did not start till it was daylight, about 6, but I went to bed and to sleep at once. It was a wee bit rough in the morning but very blue and bright and lovely. I was a little ill while getting up and doing my hair etc but quite recovered on deck, and was even able to have some breakfast before long. Of course the whole place was crowded with officers, most of them going out for the first time. Some of them were very sick, poor dears, I expect as much from nervousness as from the roughness of the sea. But they were all by way of being very cheery before they left the boat.

We had no excitements on the way and I saw nothing worthy of note – not a ship till we were well within sight of France.

We landed about 12 – the men who examined my passport told me to go by Trouville. Then another official told me certainly not to, and that it would be less trouble to stay the night in Havre. Finally I found two French girls going to Caen this way, so I decided to do the same.

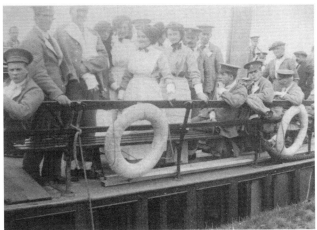

Norfolk War Hospital
patients on an outing.
(ACC 2009/103)

This boat did not start till 3.45 so I left my luggage on it, sent off my wire and had *dejeuner* at a restaurant.

It is very exciting actually being in France and seeing the things one has read of, Turcos cheering English soldiers as they march past, an English Tommy solemnly shaking hands with his host a she comes out of a pub. There seemed crowds of wounded French soldiers sitting about in the *Places*, and of course Englishmen everywhere. Havre is a jolly place with its sunny streets and all the shipping.

Now we are just outside the harbour and it is very lovely with lots of little red fishing boats. Sept 22: I will finish this in my room, at Mondeville, the next day.

My journey was not quite such a success as I imagined it was going to be. I arrived at Trouville on the most perfect afternoon and quite lost my heart to it: it was of course empty of everyone except inhabitants – wounded soldiers. I drove through it from the pier to the station in a bus, with all my baggages – then discovered that the next train to Caen did not start till about 7, and did not arrive till 11.

I went out and wired to Cousin Minnie, but they told me the chances were against the wire being delivered till next Monday, so I felt rather despondent, as my French girls told me I should never be able to find a cab to Mondeville at that hour. The train journey was so long only because we were turned out at Lisieux and had to wait two hours and a half on a most dreary platform. Luckily it was a warm and lovely night with a brilliant moon. In the train to Caen, when at last it came, I consulted a nice old man who said I had certainly better stop at the Hotel d'Angleterre.

However, at Caen, to my joy, I found Cousin Minnie waiting for me. It was most awfully good of her to have come, at that time of night, but she said directly she received my first wire, saying that I should arrive at 8, she knew I should not really manage it, as everyone was taken in in the same way.

So we drove up here in the dark and found the room looking most inviting, with tea things prepared, in case I should be starving. This morning I slept on and did not go down to the Hospital till 9.30, feeling very terrified. I am on Cousin Minnie's floor, as I had hoped. There is another girl, a Miss Gemmott or something, Cousin Minnie and myself. Ward no. 14, with 29 beds, is going to be mine especially. Things have been in great confusion today, as there have suddenly come orders that the hospital is to be *evacuee* of all patients who are fit to walk, so they are nearly all going – we are expecting new arrivals tomorrow or the next day. In my ward (!!!!!) there were no bed cases so I think they are all going except two.

There appear to be no appliances of any sort, and no water hot or cold, except what the men will kindly fetch from the kitchen in one single jug. When I first arrived this morning I had to clean up the dressing bowls and mackintoshes with only the water in a single spirit lamp! So I did a sort of dry clean with ether and carbolic. Also meth is almost impossible to get, so one cannot use a spirit lamp much. Everything is very dirty and messy but the men are delightful and I can understand them quite well. They seem very friendly, unshy and apparently very biddable.

My room is in the Villa, with everyone else's, about 10 minutes walk from the Hospital. It is on the ground floor, with great big opening windows and a parquet floor, and absolutely no bedroom furniture besides a comfortable bed with a yellow quilt. This does not matter as there is a good bathroom and plenty of washing appliances. It is really very charming and we have lovely French meals and it is so hot and sunny.

Hospital 43, Mondeville, 30 September 1915:
Our *nouveaux blesses* have not yet arrived and the men in my *Salle* are now diminished to 10, so I am able to fuss round them and lavish tenderest care on them, though I am powerless to give them clean sheets or a glass of milk even. I think they are doing well, though they have some grisly wounds. In fact the *Salle* is a horrible sight at 9 o'clock in the morning. The old man who had haemorrhage and about whom Cousin Minnie was so worried, had it again and yet again, and at last was rushed down to another hospital in Caen and operated on, but has since died, poor old man.

Mondeville, 30 October 1915:
We are going on the same as ever: the man who was X rayed was operated on this morning, and is now rather bad and in great pain: otherwise we have no one at all bad downstairs. The new doctor instead of M Leceof arrived suddenly this morning. We do not know his name yet, but he looked a fairly good natured red faced man, in a very new uniform. He has been in an ambulance, so we fear he may be rather rough and ready in his methods.

I had quite thought this Hospital had hardened me to everything and that I was getting past shocks, but imagine my feelings this morning when I saw the doctor's nailbrush calmly being used to brush a man's hair with!! Tell Doro and Kitty that and they will understand my feelings. Oh it is very deadly dull here with so little to do.

[undated]:
I am very sorry about all you tell me of Hope Burke: I had gathered from Aunt Mary's letters that things were going so smoothly. If I am to take you literally, that she danced an Irish jig, I am utterly shocked: because, as I told you when I was at home, I learnt at Thorpe how fatal it was if once a nurse began to romp in front of the men.... It is getting almost unbearable here, having nothing to do.

Mondeville, 6 December 1915:
Fancy Aunt Mary having 23 men! I cannot think where they all sleep, or where they all come from. Are they short of convalescent homes in Norfolk that they send her so many?

Joyce returned home for Christmas, then went back to France:

Mondevlle, 30 December 1915:
Here I am again, and the hospital is stark empty! I am rather sick at heart but putting a good face on the matter.... At present the hospital contains one soldier and I think seven civilians. All the hospitals in Caen are equally empty, all having been cleared at the same time. There is a new *Medecin Chef*, who is apparently very particular about cleanliness and won't allow the *Infirmiers* to be on the beds, which is good hearing.... Oh it will be dull, but anyway as you said I am at my post of duty, and wounded may arrive and then it will be too frantic.

Mondeville, 3 January 1916:
Cousin Minnie is really determined to leave on Wednesday and spends all her time in giving me last injunctions and instructions. I shall be dreadfully lost when she is gone, alone downstairs among a crowd of horrible *Infirmiers*. I only hope I shall not lose the position she has so

laboriously won. However, I fully perceive that it is my lot to stay here while she is away, even if not a single wounded man arrives.

At present we have 8 or 9 men in the downstairs wards, and none of them really in the army, but men who have been mobilised for munition work. They come from all parts of France, and are very like the others were, except that they can threaten to leave the hospital if they do not like their treatment, as they are not military. Unfortunately they need very little doing for them: two temperatures to be taken, two cups of Bovril administered and two *vont tousses* to be put on and an occasional wet dressing, is really all. Otherwise one can play games with them or give them books.

The hospital is much cleaner and tidier and there are stricter rules about smoking. I have not seen the new doctor, but the *Infirmiers* are very much afraid of him, which I am glad of.

Mondeville, 21 January 1916:
I am sorry you thought Cousin Minnie looking old and worn: as a matter of fact, this boredom that you scoff at me for talking about is, I am sure, more trying than much hard work, and I shall probably come back looking quite 'haggard'. There is little news from here. The *Medecin Chef's* wife has just arrived, and spent this morning trolling round the hospital after him, and even attended at an operation that was going on! Imagine that in an English hospital!

The nice 'well brought up' Miss Scott leaves on Wednesday. I shall quite miss her, for though she is as dull as a sheet of artificial water and has read not a book except novels, she is so obviously well brought up that I had a good deal in common with her …

Supposing no wounded have arrived, I shall think of returning in about a month's time, when Cousin Minnie will perhaps be coming back. What shall I do then? Do try to find out for me whether nurses are still needed in England, and where: I really cannot go on indefinitely waiting for this to fill up, when I think it is quite on the cards that it never fills at all. So if you meet anyone whose opinion is worth having, try to find out whether untrained nurses are still wanted …

I feel sure that there are soon going to be ructions at Kirstead, but I hope for Doro's sake not.

Mondeville, 25 January 1916:
I had a letter from Aunt Mary this morning … She gave me some family news … that Doro was suffering in silence from the dreadful troubles at Kirstead, which of course she won't speak about …

All these letters were written by Joyce to her mother. In one letter to her sister Kitty, she was very forthright about the roles that the sisters might play during the war:

Mondeville, 1 February 1916:
Dearest Kitty, Many thanks for your letter. I am heartily with you that we all ought to be doing some work, and my only trouble is to decide what it ought to be. I well know the difficulties when one is living at home! If only the family would do something drastic, and dismiss all the servants, chauffeurs and coachmen, one might really have a chance of being useful, but as things are it is not much of a war time life.

But I am afraid for myself, that I ought to stay here until Cousin Minnie, or someone else, comes back. I feel it would be too unbearable for two [the two remaining English nurses] to be left alone. But I suppose that only means staying till the end of February.

What do you say to coming and making munitions after that? I am not at all sure that this would be wise, as we have both had some nursing training, but my reasons are these:

1. I do not believe the Red X are in any need of V.A.D.s just now
2. There would be no slack times or waiting for work
3. We should be free to leave when we wished
4. I must confess I rather dread the idea of another English hospital, with sisters and all

But anyway if there should come a great rush of wounded and nurses were badly wanted again, we could both of us return to our respective hospitals whenever we wished.

What do you think?

You might anyway make some enquiries about how to apply for such work and where it is wanted and the conditions etc Doro might like to come and we could alternate, so that one was always at home.

Communicate the suggestion to the family, and see if they think it quite mad. When I am alone here, I always suspect that my decisions may be rather mad, as I have no one to talk them over with ...

I am quite horrified and miserable at hearing this evening about the great Zepp raid on England. I even wish storms and bad weather would begin again.

Inside Kirstead Auxiliary Hospital. (PD 300/41)

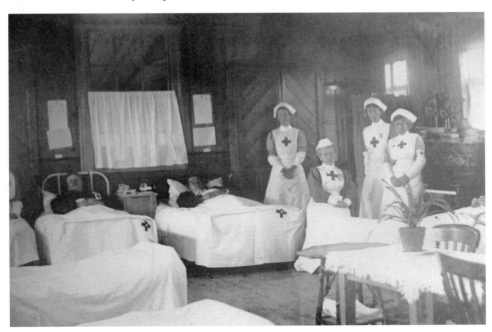

Patients and nurses
outside Kirstead Hospital.
(PD 300/41)

No follow-up letters survive, so we do not know if these plans were pursued any
further. Just a few days later, Joyce was writing again to her mother:

Mondeville, 4 February:
I was so sorry Aunt Mary is tired and worried: it is a very good thing she is shutting her
hospital for a week. I never quite understood what happened about her second nurse: didn't
Miller come back again, and if so why was not all well? But it was very silly of her not to have
used Doro and K more often, when they were so willing to go …

I suppose Cousin Minnie does not really mean to come back till the hospital fills up: she
wrote saying that perhaps I had better come home if I really wanted to do something else, but
I should hate leaving these two all alone here. Miss Walker would get so dreadfully bored, and
if one of them got ill or anything, it would be rather awful. I rather feel there ought not be less
than three of us here.

I heard yesterday that 200 wounded or chiefly ill men had arrived in Caen yesterday, so
possibly they may be filling up this part of the world again. But I feel in my inmost soul that they
might very easily leave this hospital till last, so that it would never get filled at all. It is a very
difficult matter to decide what to do. I wish military nursing was not such a waiting job.

I have not much desire to write to the Red Cross. I don't think they are short of nurses, and
if I were in England and there was a great filling up of hospitals, I could always go back to the
old NWH. Kitty could come there with me, for the matter of that. But I am afraid I am very
undecided.

Have you any first hand news of the Zeppelin raid? It is so horribly frightening, their coming
in such numbers.

Mondeville, 7 Februry:
How frightened I am to hear that the Zeppelins came right over you all. I do hope you are
being very careful not to allow a vestige of light to appear. I am so sorry for all those poor
Midland towns, all foolishly and brightly lit up, and all unsuspecting, but how I wish we could
protect ourselves somehow better …

I cannot bear the mention or thought of reprisal for air raids, nor does it seem a very feasible suggestion just at present as we have no Zeppelins, but I cannot help thinking we might defend ourselves better with more up to date aeroplanes, and might also have more attacks on Zepp sheds where they are within reach …

At present there are no signs of filling up: the doctor and his wife have gone to Paris for nearly a week, but he is said to have written somewhere or other about getting wounded sent here.

Joyce turned twenty-six while she was in Mondeville, which led to an introspective letter to her mother:

10 February:
I am awfully old am I not? It almost makes me blush because I am so much older than I feel, and I think it is most unfortunate when there is such as discrepancy between one's real age and one's felt age. In so many ways I feel younger and less sure of myself than I was five years ago. I imagine it may be a good thing insofar as it means reconsidering one's formed opinions: but I must admit I had always hoped that I should feel more comfortable in the world when I was 26, than I actually am.

How can you possibly say that economy is only a personal matter and not a national one as long as taxes are paid? I marvel at you! I marvel that anyone should be so entirely lacking in social sense as you pretend to be! But this matter of economy is of course nothing to do with feelings or sentiment, but is simply a matter of common sense and figures. I almost blush to write the much used arguments: when the country is short of labour, how can you justify its use in providing you with unnecessaries? When all transport is a problem, especially from overseas, each person who eats an unnecessary orange must make a difference to the supply of war materials, or else to the prices of necessaries. It all seems as clear as daylight, but horribly hard to act on.

I suppose, then, I had better stay on here, for a bit anyway. As you say, it would be most annoying if the hospital got busy immediately after I left. Cousin Minnie shows no desire to fix a date for her coming back, and I suppose that if I am going to stay here, she had better not come yet awhile, as that would make less to do than ever.

I am a miserable exile, that is all.

I am much amused to hear about Rachel, and her father's rescuing her from that awful place where there was no chance of washing. What is the other place she means to go to? Another nursing home for army horses?

23 February:
I am rather sorry Kitty means to go and be a stable boy with Rachel, as she still gets so tired with riding. But I expect they would rather have a jolly time together, if they go. It is a great thing that there should be two of them, and I expect after her late experiences, Ray will be more careful where she goes.

I still wish Doro would come here, in spite of her scouts, though I know they are both important and engrossing. But of course if she says she will come she must stick to it, or it would add terribly to the muddle of finding people to come here.

29 February:

This fighting is very terrible: two days ago, in spite of reassuring articles in the paper, I thought I detected attempts to prepare one's mind for the worst, and I imagined that Verdun was going to fall. But now I think the news is much better: all we really need is that the enemy should not advance: if we succeed in holding out it will be a big victory. Oh these are exciting times: this fighting, horrible and terrible as it is, seems to bring the end so much nearer … I have had 13 men in my ward at the moment, of which I am rather proud. The rheumatic man has wonderfully recovered, but I have had two rather ill with 'colique' needing frequent hot water bottles and hot compresses.

4 March:

We have heard nothing further about wounded, and they seem to have stopped coming into Caen … Yesterday we got permission and were taken over the works here, which was most interesting. They no longer make any small shells here, except just to finish off their contracts, and are making the most enormous ones. We saw some giants, a yard and a half high, and followed them through all their stages, from the making of the moulds to the pouring in of the red hot metal, and then the lathing and the putting on of the cotton bands, to the final weighing and testing.

Their output is not very big now, but it is increasing. I knew so many of the men, who had either been in the hospital or had come up as outpatients that it was especially amusing. Everywhere one seemed to be greeted by polite salutes and well known smiling faces. A lot of the men grumble tremendously at the way they are treated at the works, though, and say no proper precautions are taken against accidents, and so much is done by favouritism, which I believe is true. Everyone seems to agree that a man who is not really a mechanic or a metal worker really can get into works like these by knowing or being related to a manager or a deputy. Then of course, when they get here, they keep the others back by their slow work, and make mistakes that lead to accidents.

6 March:

Of course I am absolutely *accablee* today to hear Cousin Minnie won't be able to get back yet awhile! It really is rather a knock down blow. Talk about responsibility: I shall be overwhelmed by it: I shall probably be the only person who has ever worked on the bottom floor, or knows the doctor, or anything. And you don't seem to realise that instead of allowing me to come back it fixes me out here. I shall not possibly be able to leave when we are anyhow one short on the staff, and when no one else knows the ways of downstairs or can keep things right for CM when she returns. I suppose now I shall have to stay here till some time in the summer, when, if everything is in proper swing, I may be able to get someone to take my place.

To add one thing to another, we find today that it was an entirely false rumour that wounded had arrived in Caen, so most likely all those hospitals have still to be filled up before we are. I think we are very fortunate to have our old munition workers to go on with.

10 March:

I am now beginning to wonder whether we shall ever get busy. I suppose there is really no doubt of it, but it seems as far off as ever. It was a false rumour that the Caen hospitals had filled: they are still quite empty. But they say that the hospitals near the front are all full, and also those at Havre.

Yesterday we went to the Church Army Hospital at Caen, and they are in just the same plight as we. It is no use asking the doctor, as you keep suggesting: they know exactly as much and as little as we do, and are only too willing to tell anything they know. You need not imagine we are much afraid of our doctors here: we always walk through doors in front of them, instead of behind, and ask them anything we want to know.

Joyce stayed on through the summer, even after Cousin Minnie had returned, then suddenly left Mondeville to travel back from Ditchingham: so suddenly that when she got there, her mother had gone away to stay with a relative!

Ditchingham Hall, 12 November:
My decision to come home was the suddenest thing ever known. I had not a thought of it till the middle of last Tuesday morning. Then we had heard from the inspecting general that very likely there would be no wounded arriving till January ... Then C[ousin] M[innie] suddenly said to me that I had better go, as obviously I was wasting time and money out there. And it really seemed that I had better profit by the general slackness to come, and would make no difference to the others. There was not much time to think about it, as I wanted to travel with the ill Miss Metcalf and Sister Carter who were leaving on Wednesday, so I rushed off and got my passport *vised* and my box packed at once.

I am home for a month probably, but if they are still empty at the end of that time and if it makes no difference to the others getting away, I might stay over Christmas. On the other hand if wounded arrive, Cousin Minnie will wire and I must go back at once. I had to promise to her most solemnly that I would come back in any case ... Anyway it is ripping being back home. Do come back quickly, dearest. Of course I do not really feel I have earned a holiday yet, but it was silly staying out there and doing quite nothing.

The letters end at this point, so we do not know if Joyce ever returned to France. The convalescent homes at Hedenham and Kirstead continued to serve the wounded throughout the war. There is now a plaque at Hedenham Hall, which includes the words: 'By God's blessing, nearly 800 wounded men found healing and rest under this roof.' Joyce Carr never married; she died in Norfolk in December 1973 at the age of eighty-three.

Joyce Carr was clearly an independent young woman, used to travelling. A younger girl, Ruth Hewetson, left Norwich High School for Girls in March 1918 to join a Voluntary Aid Detachment. She was sent to a hospital on Salisbury Plain, leaving her Norfolk home for the first time.

Ruth Hewetson, Fargo Hospital, March 1918:
My very dearest Mother & Father.
Here I am!!! I'll start from when I left Father. I had a nice journey down – the country was so pretty – I hardly read at all & I managed the change quite easily. When I arrived at Amesbury a Corporal touched me on the shoulder & said 'Are you for Fargo' so I said 'Yes'; he collected all my belongings & took them & me out to a Red X van (labelled 'for infectious cases only') put us all in behind & set off. We're 6 miles from the Station & I had a very jolly ride feeling most amused at myself. When I arrived there was no formality at all – I went almost immediately

Patients and nurses outside
Kirstead Hospital. (PD 300/41)

into the kitchen & had a lovely tea while all other G.S. Members dropped in & out. They are so nice & nearly all very Irish. (so Mother, do tell me about my Irish relations & tendencies!) Since tea I've unpacked. We are in a sort of hutment camp. I'm in a hut divided off into dear little cubicles by curtains. With a passage w' stoves in round wh: we sit. (I'd like a small vase – then later you can send me a few flowers now & then.) The photos & silver dressing table things look so nice. It is a beautifully warm hut. I think I am here for a year – so that will please you. Evidently it does not sound like 'abroad' yet. My Work is a hut like this used by 11 Sisters who are on night duty, I get up at 5.30 (!!!!). have an early small breakfast & get their rooms done by 9 when they come in to go to sleep. I am entirely responsible but all I do is slops(!) dusting & sweeping (please send a few hints re proper way of doing a washstand!).

Ruth wrote home every week; I have transcribed her fascinating and important letters in a book published by the Norfolk Record Society.

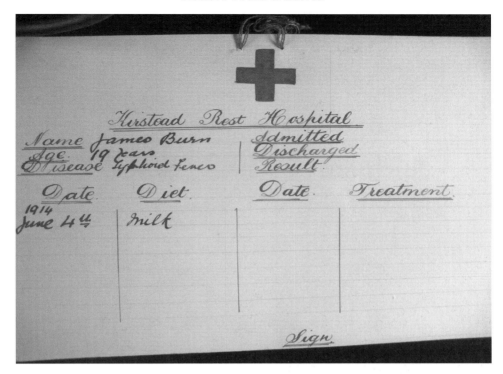

Patients' record cards, Kirstead
Auxiliary Hospital. (PD 300/42)

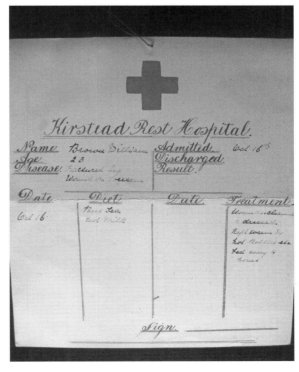

3

A NORFOLK NURSE'S DIARY

The majority of Norfolk nurses naturally stayed within their home county, working in one of the many convalescent homes that sprang up during the war. Edith Upcher was the youngest of four children of Henry Morris Upcher, 'squire' of Sheringham Hall, and his wife, Maria. Born 2 August 1877, she was christened Caroline Edith Sparke Upcher, but was known as Edith to family and friends. She kept a diary of her time spent working in a Sheringham hospital – this was Knowelside on Cliff Road, with forty-five beds. Her account, with its stories of invasion scares, Zeppelins and mines, is an evocative description of Sheringham in the war years. In the diary, Edith frequently mentions 'Lily': this is the family nickname of her elder sister Louisa. The sisters were unmarried and lived in the family home at Sheringham Hall.

25 February 1916:
This should have begun Aug 1st 1914, but like many other resolutions is somewhat late in being carried out. Having given up all ideas of keeping a war diary the clouding in of events have compelled me to begin this so late in the day. As if possible I intend to enter the daily happenings, & to recall those which are passed – No one is advised to read but may be permitted to do so (if they can) and have plenty of time to waste.

Perhaps the Zeppelin night makes a Landmark of War mark at which to begin. Jan 31st 1916. Feeling weary tumbled on to my bed after late lunch on return to Hospital & slept like a log. Wake up room rather unusually dark. Light came in: 'is it tea time yet & time to get up?'

'Tea time & an hour after and didn't you hear that horrid thing go over?' There being only one 'horrid thing that goes over' I got out of bed dressed & went to drawing room for cold tea Father Mother & Lily quite 'normal conditions' I could see, having heard nothing. The servants had heard the Zeppelin & also seen it going quite low over the wood near the house.

I made no remark, but in an hour's time heard a suspicious purring of engines. Tho' not like the thrusting machine noises of Jan 1915. I felt sure of Zepp machinery. Lil, Father & I exchanged

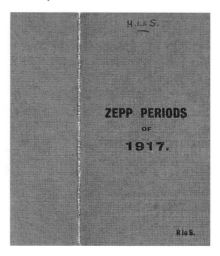

Probable Raid Periods denoted in Red (New Moons heavy type).											
JAN.	FEB.	MAR.	APL.	MAY	JUNE	JULY	AUG.	SEP.	OCT.	NOV.	DEC.
15	13	13	11	12	11	10	8	6	7	7	6
16	14	14	12	13	12	11	9	7	8	8	7
17	15	15	13	14	13	12	10	8	9	9	8
18	16	16	14	15	14	13	11	9	10	10	9
19	17	17	15	16	15	14	12	10	11	11	10
20	18	18	16	17	16	15	13	11	12	12	11
21	19	19	17	18	17	16	14	12	13	13	12
22	20	20	18	19	18	17	15	13	14	14	13
23	21	21	19	20	19	18	16	14	15	15	14
24	22	22	20	21	20	19	17	15	16	16	15
25	23	23	21	22	21	20	18	16	17	17	16
26	24	24	22	23	22	21	19	17	18	18	17
27	25	25	23	24	23	22	20	18	19	19	18
28	26	26	24	25	24	23	21	19	20	20	19
29	27	27	25	26	25	24	22	20	21	21	20
30	28	28	26	27	26	25	23	21	22	22	21
31	...	29	27	28	27	26	24	22	23	23	22
...	...	30	28	29	28	27	25	23	24	24	23
...	...	31	29	30	29	28	26	24	25	25	24

All Raids have occurred with a light wind, practically on a level or rising barometer, from 30° upwards.

Predicting Zeppelin raids. (LEST supplementary 34/9)

glances. The noise became more distant, seemed following the coast for a bit. Then – Crash. Bang. Shake. A loud explosion. & every door & window in the house struggling to break free, another & another – then louder. Mother thought first of a Naval engagement but we told her it was Zeppelins and one at first thought of our guns firing at it. Burford soon came along & we knew that Bombs were being hurled from the sky some where in Holt direction. A lull in the banging then Harman's quiet voice at the door asking 'what about the jewellery' very thoughtful but what a comparative value jewellery seemed to have, when one felt what are those bombs doing and whose turn next?? Another series of explosions then quiet for the rest of the evening. We heard later on that they were Bayfield way.

In the quiet of one's room how strange it seemed and sleep not so near as usual. Nearly midnight, imagination or noise. Gradually growing to reality of returning night monsters of prey. Where had they been what had they done, would they have any spare bombs to leave as mementos – and would the longed for gale arise and dispel the fog and prevent the coming of the iron cross of wickedness.

I February:
Reports as usual only more so. Everyone claimed that it 'went right over my house'. Hospital calm tho' the locals had been a little excited.

Busy morning with out patients. No papers in but reports many. 'Bayfield Hall – blown to bits', 'Great damage at Norwich' etc etc. Real truth being that 30 bombs were dropt at Bayfield Lodge hoping no doubt that it was the airdrome. Windows of house broken, barn damaged, and forge blown to bits. Many dropped in fields. A row of 8 large holes in which 22 men could stand. (This stated by the 62nd who marched over to see it. Many blistered feet in consequence among the elders of 39 - military age) Report told of aircraft party having left on their large light and finding "things too hot for them" fled to Holt, leaving their searchlight turned on Holt Lodge.

Zepps reported about again on Tuesday night. Not confirmed. More tales about as to the lowness of the Zepp as it came over the cliffs and hovered about.

Reveille, Holt. (MC 2043/2/90)

There were more rumours of Zeppelins later in the month.

8 February:
N. Trendell to tea. Story of his visit to war offices at Burlington [a large hotel on the sea front] – History repeating itself 2 ladies (on arrival of new regiment each time) demanding 2 rooms. One facing the sea, the other the back of the Hotel – suspiciously like spies – but after a time proved to be officers' wives coming to stay - tame finish!

Story of YMCA man being taken to see Dutch prize ship with 125 bags of revolvers and 15 bags of ammunition taken off at Dover. In spite of Captain protesting they were not on board. N. Trendell's dream of Zeppelin dragging a large train with 2 engines then thousands of paper boats filled with children floating down from it.

9 February:
Heard great buzzing while walking across Park 3 P.M. Could see nothing but a snow white sea plane probably German was seen going past same time a raid was being made in Kent.

10 February:
Henry and Nina came to stay. Mr Sandison R.G.A to billet but only in to tea & then slept up by the Weybourne guns. Zepp-like night.

11 February:
Mr Sandison came in to late breakfast reported of zepps about from 7-12 PM. but further north. Stormy day. Lunch with Molly for her birthday.

N. Fitch told of girl who lost her power of speech when she saw the zepps. Field day on cliffs. N. Fitch insisted on going through the sentry's gate taking congregation of 1 with him.

Mother & I to Brab fairly excited by the Zeppelin. Mr Flowerdew: 'There was an excitement up here the other night there bang bang and they came running in to put out my light and said that was the Germans about and that was only the wind (dead calm) blowing the roof off, so and so's barn door down the lane, don't they talk a lot of rubbish telling us it was the Germans.' Another tale to Lily on next visit 'My Jemmie he was a solider and he went to the war but he never got hit 'cause he hopped every time he see a shot comin' at him, he hopped, and they all said 'well done Jemima' and then he hopped again when there was the South African war.'

12 February:
Henry and Nina left by 8.50 train Mr Sandison in to breakfast having slept 'on the guns'. He went to Woolwich for gunnery course. A lovely day. Guns fired from Links but as Lily & I went into Cromer did not hear them.

There were yet more Zeppelin scares later.

21 February:
Stayed at Hospital for lunch and went to station to meet Dove and take her to Kylemore to practise songs. With Mr Warren. At station heard of Zeppelins off the coast. As we drove off loud report, and saw smoke puff in the air over Grand Hotel – everyone gazing at the sky. In a few seconds another. We settled they were clearing the guns in readiness for the zepps as after scanning the skies no enemy aircraft was visible. We also calculated that Zepps 130 miles east of Mundesley at 9.30 would give time for the YMCA Hut to be opened before the raiders appeared.

Took Aunt Laura home, Mr Warren to the Hut. Speeches by various secretaries. The Bishop of Norwich made opening speech. Father proposed vote of thanks in good speech and roused the dull assembly by quoting from Dutt's book about the request for guns & ammunition for the defence of the town in 16.

Cousin Digby thanked the donors and when everyone had thanked everyone else the proceedings grew a little more lively with songs from Dove, and a few hoarse failures from Mr Allen Dale. Unfortunately the show was made into a helpers benefit instead of a welcome to soldiers very disappointing. Mr Warren was due at guns at 5 & owing to Zepp scare had to be punctual so we drove him in car to Weybourne Hills – Lovely sunset glow.

(After all the rush, the guns were out walking & did not return for some time). After tea Lily Dove & I walked up hill to watch gorgeous sunset and lights and pick pink Rhododendrons.

Every where looked the very picture of peace. The Zepp scare seemed to have turned down and the 'guns' were the rockets calling the Lifeboat to a ship on the sands which got off long before the Lifeboat could get to her. Why she ever got on in a dead calm and clear day was the mystery.

A few days later, rumours spread around Sheringham that the Germans were invading.

24 February:
Good deal of agitation about. Many soldiers on Links and round Hospital. Found out from outpatient that a landing was expected. All the soldiers had been out all night & not come in for morning rations. – The lifeboat had gone out to ship in distress off Wells and had not been

heard of since. One took this quite calmly but found out that the inmates were dreadfully unnerved and expecting bombardment invasion and all the horrors of war at any minute. Hunt could not stop talking about it & hung around for company – looking untold things all the time, Miss Gully & I at last got him to smile again. Le Gros came with wide open eyes to announce that Germans had landed at Weybourne! 'How many?' 'Ah that's the worst of it no one knows & they are in Khaki & it will be a very difficult thing to find them among the other soldiers.' 'But it is quite impossible.' 'No not at all, & they are so clever' & the Lifeboat has not come back. That is often out for many hours if it has to take a boat in to Yarmouth or Lowestoft. NO it is a ruse of the Germans to get it out & take it (Further report said that the Germans in Khaki having landed were going about shaking hands with soldiers with the other hand knifing them!)

One after another the men came in with the same tale, always ending in the same awestruck voices. But the Lifeboat has not been heard of yet.

We watched with interest the many soldiers coming & going and doing much more business-like sentry work being under the eyes of the various officers who appeared very important discussing the situation on the tennis lawn by the cliff dugouts. At intervals despatches were handed them but all the while those soldiers not actually on duty were making enormous Swiss rolls of snow about 2 feet wide and rolling them round & round the tennis court till they were almost as high as themselves. A barrow was dragged up the hill by 5 soldiers. Rations we thought but only more coal for the dugout fire – As it happened there were a most unusual amount of ships hanging about all the morning. As we were looking at them we saw one of the soldiers from the Hospital hoisting the Union Jack & the Red Cross Flag. He had got leave to do this to calm his feelings – but it had the contrary effect on most of them as they again came to pour out their fears that when we are bombarded – 'I'm sorry for Sheringham when that happens they will at once fire on the Red Cross Flag, as they always do.'

About 11 o ck a Sergeant (an out-patient) came in to say that there had come an order of 'Normal Conditions' so the soldiers gradually dispersed but the excitement that 'the lifeboat has not come home' still prevailed.

During the day the fisherman became very uneasy at not hearing of her whereabouts, but at about 11.20 a telephone message came through that after a very stormy cold time she had got the ship safely to Grimsby. On the way the hawser had broken two or 3 times, & the ship was so down at the bows with water that she nearly went under in the Humber. The Lifeboat returned safely the following Sunday evening at 6 PM but the German spy idea was so firmly rooted in the military brain that when she returned the trenches were manned and Mr Page (Lifeboat secretary) was stationed on the beach to identify every member of the crew as he left the boat, loaded rifles being ready if an unknown face had appeared. Later we heard that on the Friday night of the scare, the boat being called out the same night, that orders were given to fire on any boat which attempted to land on any part of the beach. When those in authority were asked how about the Lifeboat oh they forgotten about that – so other orders had to be issued to except the Lifeboats.

When the fisherman went to the Boat to launch her they were only allowed across the cliffs with a military escort.

After work finished at Hospital, paddled down to lunch at Lodge. The Town was quite calm. Report only reached home of agitation along the coast at 1 ock. The military alertness spread all along the East Coast. Shall we ever hear if there was any foundation in the Reports?

In March, there was further drama in the little seaside town when a floating mine came ashore:

Saturday 11 March:

At 5 past 8, a resounding bang and windows rattled furiously of course no one's suggestions were the right ones. A floating mine had come ashore it was seen for 2 hours but no steps were taken to prevent disaster – Reports as usual. 'They' had telephoned to Lowestoft for instructions & received none. 'It was too rough for any boat to get out to it.' None of the fishermen dared have touched it – etc etc – anyhow, the inevitable had happened and the mine had burst. The spot it chose was the Town drain pipe – and here it did its worst though mercifully so much less than if it had met its end a few minutes sooner and not a soul was hurt or even touched by the portions of pipe, mine, stones, which were flying incredible distances into the town.

The inhabitants, being told of its nearness to the beach and the likelihood of its bursting, assembled to look at it, and were allowed to do so unmolested. The desire for breakfast at the magic hour of 8 A.M. proved stronger even than curiosity and 8.5 saw everyone seated round their breakfast tables, safely housed when the crash came. The moment that all danger was passed the front was strictly guarded and no one allowed to venture near.

Windows broken wholesale, 3 at the Hospital any amount down Cliff Road. The large plate glass in Mrs Anderson's 2 shops, a large piece of drain pipe picked up outside Chapman's shop. Beach stones & bits of mine and drain thrown great distances, one large piece near the railway bridge at end of Beeston Lane. Mrs Lucas' house the Mo badly broken about, the burst having taken place quite near. All the windows along the Front broken. Birrell's house according to Gofather Pegg [a local fisherman] was lifted out of the ground 8 inches & went back again – 'I don't think I could bear that again' – All the day he ran about carrying a bottle of medicine from which he drank at intervals. Every window broken. Mr Underhill's house suffered a good deal at least 10 windows gone. Some blown in & some blown out, but as the boys were all at breakfast none were touched. They would otherwise have been playing in the yard where masses of pieces fell & were deeply inbedded in the ground N.H is much given to 'pooh-pooh' everything. At breakfast, Mrs H 'There is a mine coming in which may explode at any minute.' Mr H 'Pooh' – – Bang – – and it had happened. One little boy inclined to get weepy. Mrs H, 'Now laddie, I told you that there was a mine going to explode, it has just happened so there is no need to be frightened for it is all over.'

As it was a stormy morning, Mrs Green's children were not spinning tops on a hard piece of ground in the garden: a large piece of metal was found in the spot.

Mr Craske heard that a mine was likely to explode. So went to his wife to tell her to get up. She dressed & went down stairs. After the explosion they went up to find on her pillow a large piece of metal.

Many like instances of wonderful escapes both true 'They says.'

The excitement was to find bits of the mine as it was said in the event of it being an English mine – the Government would have to pay damages.

Brundall. (Courtesy of Chris Basey)

Rumours of Zeppelin raids and invasion scares continued throughout March:

Friday 17 March:
St Patricks Day. Shamrocks from Dublin As I was sweeping the dining room after breakfast I expressed a wish that the windows broken by the mine bursting should be mended as being boarded up made the room so gloomy. A minute after a hideous chimpanzee-like face appeared at the open windows and a man began to climb in at the open window saying in the very broadest drawling Norfolk 'He that is not of the sheep cometh not in at the door but enters in some other way.' Fincham came to clean mend the broken panes, so tho' not of the sheep was welcome.

He told us that Zepps had been about & that Yarmouth had been bombarded the night before – that part anyhow was untrue.

Tuesday 21 March:
Wet all day. Hospital – morning. Great reports of sea battle off Newcastle – varying number as to ships sent to the bottom. Some said 17 German Battleships and 3 submarines. The Hindenburg down etc etc. – Then others – that our ships were downed & no German ones, the Lion at the bottom. Various other badly damaged brought to Newcastle. Then of many German sailors brought in as prisoners and others buried in a cemetery near N/C.

Talked with Simms as to duration of war – He said he hoped it would not end yet – as it could not be really well finished yet – and it would not be fair on them after all they had gone through and or for the women who had gone through such agonies. They would only find that their grandchildren would be going through it again.

Two new guns (Cliffs?)

Wednesday 22 March:
Very cold day. With sleet showers. Gunners out all day on long marches, officers in consequence very tired & sleepy.

Thursday 23 March:
Cold but not so showery.

At Hospital discussed in the event of invasion that the Hospital men to be returned to Norwich (how?!) and that the detachment takes work at a dressing station 8 miles behind firing line. Nurses to volunteer for the work. In case of bombardment the Hospital might have to be used first as a dressing station (if it was left standing!). Masses of minesweepers 40 at a time working about all the morning. Olive Ashby came in with tale of 10 German sea planes about – in fact just arrived.

In spite of these dangers, the hospital remained open until 31 January 1919, by which time 957 wounded soldiers had passed through.

4

LETTERS FROM PATIENTS

Some families in large residences also devoted themselves to nursing, sometimes throwing open their own houses to wounded soldiers. There were around sixty of these auxiliary hospitals in Norfolk. The soldiers who passed through one of these, Buckenham Tofts, wrote back to the hospital in appreciation, and these letters give an insight into their lives after they left the institution. The commandant of Buckenham

Nurses and patients at Buckenham Tofts. (MC 84/206)

Tofts was Lady Margaret Amherst, the widow of Lord Amherst of Hackney, who had died in 1909. The practical work was done by their unmarried daughters, especially Florence and Sybil. Like so many upper-class families, they had experienced personal tragedy: Lord William Cecil Amherst, husband of the eldest daughter, Mary, had been killed at the Battle of the Aisne in 1914. This was one of the smallest of the hospitals; it opened on 1 January 1916 with just twenty beds. As the letters show, the Amherst sisters kept in touch with their ex-patients, often sending them tobacco and other small gifts.

Letters From Soldiers in France

Private Frederick Billman, France:

Miss Amherst, I am taking great pleasure in writing this letter to you to return best thanks to you, the dowager lady, and the other Miss Amhersts, for the excellent parcel I received this noon-time from you. Nothing could have been better and I am so grateful to you. As I do not smoke much it gave me great satisfaction to distribute the cigarettes among my chums, many of whom miss a smoke more than anything. I had just used my last piece of soap, so yours saved me the trouble of getting more from these French shops. Tonight I am making some soup with some of the tablets and – well everything is so delightfully useful that I cannot mention one in particular. I will just mention a little incident that happened soon after the parcel arrived (also I had three letters, so I am by no means a lonely soldier). I had opened the parcel and my letters, and was proudly showing them all round when the 'Alarm' sounded. When this happens we have to turn out in full marching order, as we may be moving off – or it may be only a rehearsal. But all the same I scrapped my things all together, put them in my valise and turned out less than ten minutes all ready for any emergency, and after all it was only a test, so it ended A1 though the excitement ran high. Now I will say a little about my journey here. I left a southern port last Monday week at [censored], had a nice [censored] voyage and landed safely on Tuesday morning. I was with the Transport so had plenty of work loading and unloading mules etc. We went into a rest camp for a few hours, left thee at midnight to have a [censored] train ride, which landed us in a small village. One night here in barns etc, then a [censored] route march to another village where we spent two days and nights in sheds and barns, during which time it rained all the time. Then last Saturday we left there in the pouring rain for a fresh billet, and since then have been living in a village schoolroom, where we were waiting for the order to move on, as we are still several miles from the firing line. Hence the alarm I mentioned previous. We are enjoying lovely weather and if it gets no worse we shall take no harm. So at last I am doing a little bit for Home and King.

Private J. Armiger, France, 25 February 1917:

To the Dowager Lady Amherst of Hackney,

Madam, I have to thank you for your kindness in sending me the knitted woollen wrapper & cocoa & oxo tablets which I received yesterday, they will come [in] useful. We have had some sharp frosts & cold weather, but it is now much milder although we are at present getting very little sun. We have had a spell in the trenches & are having a short rest. We had our blankets & clothing disinfected today & have been & had a shower-bath, so feel much fresher & clean & comfortable.

From John Tiscom, in the trenches, France:

To the Dowager Lady Amherst of Hackney,

My lady, I now take the opportunity to write and thank your Ladyship for the parcel I received safely, which I appreciated very much.

We have been in the firing line all this week but expect to return to our rest camp in a day or so.

The weather is intensely hot, which is just satisfactory for the harvesters.

What splendid work our Navy have been doing, it was cheering to here yesterday of the four German troopships being sunk on their way to the Gallipoli peninsula, also to hear of the two Cruisers successfully shelling the Turkish forts, the only thing wanted now is for Germany to join in, which would soon settle [the war].

Private H. Lusher, British Expeditionary Force, France:

Many thanks for your kind and welcome parcel which I received today, I enjoyed the smokes ever so much. It brought to my mind the old village far away but I hope I shall have the pleasure of seeing it again some day and the friends which have been so kind to me.

Private W. G. Thompson, BEF, France, 12 September 1915:

I now take pleasure in writing to thank you so very much for the parcel which I received quite safe, on the 11th inst and I was very pleased with the same and we quite enjoyed the cigarettes. I am very sorry that I have not written to you before but we have been very busy since we have been out here, and then I was in hospital for three weeks and I have been back only a few days but I am feeling quite well again now, so I hope you will forgive me for not writing to your more often.

I have been in the trenches eight times now but it has been very quiet up to the present and we are back for a short rest now. But of course we are getting fit now to make an advance and so we get plenty of training. My mate and I and I are both 'Bomb Throwers' and we will try our best to make Fritz jump when we go up the line again.

Letters From Soldiers in Britain

Private G. Clover, Margate, 25 February 1916:

Just a line to let you know I am having a fine time and my people were pleased also surprised to see me home yesterday except my father and he came to the station to meet me. It had been snowing all the way down the line but not as bad as Norfolk, and I quite enjoyed my ride to the car yesterday. I am trying to get some fish for you but I don't know if I can manage it as the boats are not going out. Give my kindest regards to all the boys, also I thank you very much for the way you have looked after [me] and all that you have done.

Private G. Clover, Fort George, Scotland, 7 March 1916:

Just a line letting you know that I arrived back on Saturday afternoon. On Sunday I had to report sick and went before the M. O. on Monday getting home service for a time … I am going on very nicely now for I think the Margate air has done me a lot of good, but my feet have been a bit worse since I have been back in Scotland, that is because of the snow and cold, for it has been snowing every day since I have been up hear.

A ward in the NWH. (ACC 2009/103)

Australian patients in the NWH. (ACC 2013/320)

I have finished the jacket so I have been sending it down to ask you if you would put it together and to see if it is right. Also I have enough wool left to make another scarf so would you let me know if I should make it now and send it down with the other as that is all I have to do to pass the time away.

Did Sister Ethel tell you my service as I was just sending to her when your card came, for I enlisted on 29 April 1915 and [spent] about ten or twelve weeks in France. Please give my kindest regard to Miss Florence, the sisters, nurses and all the boys, also Lady Amherst and Mrs Lancaster.

Letters From Soldiers in other Hospitals

Private H. Robinson, Red Cross, Attleborough:
Dear Matron, I am very pleased to say I have received your parcel for which I thank you very much. The glass which you enclosed is a valuable asset for shaving, as there is only one glass in the whole hospital as far as I can see.

Private Twigg, no date or address:
Dear Nurse Sybil, Just a line, hoping this will find you quite well. Did you finish my portrait and is the Photos out yet, the one you took on the day we left. Have you ordered those paints yet. Shall be glad to see you again. No Tobacco issue here as at Buckenham.

Private F. H. Twigg, Red Cross Hospital, Bodney, King's Lynn, 24 April 1916:
I am to have milk food and get out as much as possible. It will be alright if this weather lasts. Please will you bring with you on Tuesday the prescription of my cough mixture. I went to the Communion Service yesterday morning and the evening prayers at 6. There was no 11 service as the Vicar has two churches to go to, but on ordinary Sundays there is a service here at 10. The church is very plain, no organ, but was beautifully decorated. There was about 30 took communion, so was very good according to the parish. If Nurse Partridge is at the hospital today please tell her I will write in a few days.

Private F. H. Twigg, Red Cross Hospital, Bodney, King's Lynn, 26 April 1916:
Just a line hoping you are quite well. I am going on as well as can be expected. If the fine weather continues it will be alright. There is only one fault with this hospital and that is that the sanitary conditions are not suitable for a hospital. Received books for scraps, with many thanks for same. Please will you send me the prescription of that paste and I will try and make me some myself. When you come across the pictures, if you are sending them please send mine to Sheerness, but if someone is bringing them it will not matter … The Sergt seems greatly dissatisfied with this place. I hear you have had a visit of one of the Zep. I believe there was a battle off the E coast yesterday, and the rebellion at Dublin, which is very bad news.

Private Twigg, Red Cross Hospital, Bilney Manor:
Received your kind gift with many thanks for same. I was greatly disappointed over yesterday's affair, especially as the Matron denied having heard from you. She must have had your letter to have answered it. Can you wonder now the Sergt and Sturgess leaving so soon. Why did she

Bracondale patients take the Norfolk air. (ACC 2009/296)

not say she did not want us to go and [have] done with it. Have not been out once since I been here. I am sorry now that she is doing this for making money, she thinks more of her churches and dogs than us. It is enough to make anyone fed up. You have to provide everything yourself from paper to tobacco. I shall clear out as soon as I can after this. I wrote to Bogg on Sunday.

P.S. Had a letter yesterday from Sis. Joy, she is out of a place. She went to one on Saturday but they wanted her to go back to caps and be called Nurse but she was not having it.

Private Twigg, Red Cross Hospital, Bilney Manor, 18 May 1916:
I am about the same, do not seem to improve. I asked the Doctor on Tuesday to let me go back to Thorpe, so as I could have the open air treatment, but he said he will have my expectoration exam[ined] again first. I told him I was sent home to go to a Sanatorium but he said that T.B. could [not] be found.

Private F. H. Twigg [no address]:
Received your letter with many thanks for same. I am about the same. Please will you send me that prescription of that paste as I will try and get some made up here as there is nothing here at present in that form. I have had 2 bad nights, brought up blood again the last 3 mornings. I think we shall all be glad when this Hospital moves to the other place. I hope you will soon be successful in getting another place [for me] as this is not what it ought to be for a Hospital. My opinion is that they are doing it for the money. They do not take much interest in the work and do not mix with us … we get no rides [out] so do not get any change.

Private F. H. Twigg, Ward 5A, Norfolk War Hospital, Thorpe, Norwich, 13 June 1916:
Yours to hand with many thanks. Thanks very much for Tobacco. I have been in bed for a week, my chest has been so painful and my cough does not seem to improve. Bogg told me about the picture, thanks very much for sending mine home. Had another letter from Sister Joy, she starts day duty on Friday. On Tuesday next is the Sports Day.

There was a concert in the Hall this afternoon but I did not go, I thought it would be too close. It would have been on the Recreation Ground if the weather had [been better]. I hope we shall soon get a change, no chance of me getting any better while it lasts. On Thursday the Nurses play another match with Patients who have not played cricket before, to wear skirts and sun hats. Bogg still going on alright, you would see the difference in him.

Private Twigg, Thorpe War Hospital, no date:
I am about the same, no information. I had a chat with the Sister. She says (result of XRay, both lungs affected), if they could find T.B. I should go at once to a Sanatorium in Kent. I shall be here a week or so and then go before a Medical Board. I still bring up blood nearly every morning now. I have lost 3 pounds this week, now only 9 stone 3 pounds, I have lost 7½ pounds since I left you. Bogg is as well as can be expected, he is back in this ward again. He wishes to thank you for Photos. He will write in a few days. On Sunday afternoon I went to Yarmouth with one of the Canadian Artillery and another patient. The invitation was one from one of the directors of an Electrical Engineering firm. Yesterday some of us went to the Dean of Norwich for tea. We had a look around the Cathedral which is very decent for its age, 800 years old. On Saturday last the Doctors played a cricket match with the patients, the Doctors being the winners. There was a Regimental Bagpipe Band in attendance. Today the Doctors play the Norwich Grammar School.

Private D. Bogg, Ward 3A, Norfolk War Hospital, Thorpe, Norwich:
Dear Matron, Just a few lines hoping this will find you quite well as this leaves me fairly.

Oh this place is a Prison to your lovely Hospital. I was in agony last night and they took no notice of me. I have had nothing done for me since I have been here so I am getting out as soon as possible. No sugar in our drink. No. Dear Matron, I must thank you very much for your kindness and looking after me as you have done. I hope you had a nice time in the city with sister. I suppose she has gone now. Please give my kind regards to all left in the hospital. I have not much news this time will write more next time.

E. Bogg (sister of Private Bogg) Luton Hoo, Beds:
Dear Miss Amherst,
Mum wishes me to write to thank you very much for the information chart you sent for Dave. It is very kind of you to send it and I am sure he will like it ever so much. We had a letter from him yesterday he has had the Xrays on him again but he didn't know the verdict yet. I don't know if he has written and told you that we have two cousins in the hospital where he is so it won't seem quite as strange to him will it? One is a nurse and the other helps with the work.

The Zepps haven't been any more. We were turned out of the works at 11.45 on Weds night and told to go into the bomb proof rooms, but I don't think they came anywhere near

Buckenham Tofts. (MC 84/206)

Luton. We are doing three weeks night work. We have to start from home about 6 o'clock and it is nearly nine o'clock when we get home in the morning. But we don't mind it a bit, it is nice to feel you are helping.

Wishing to thank you for all your kindness to my brother, I remain, yours humbly, E Bogg.

Private D. Bogg, Ward 5A, Norfolk War Hospital, Thorpe, Norwich:
To the Hon, Margaret Amherst of Hackney,
Many thanks for your kind letter of yesterday, and also for sending me my handkerchief. I left 3 of them behind me at Buckenham. What awful weather we are having, raining every day and night. I am getting on fairly well again now. Twigg is fairly well but has been in bed a few days. Father is having good luck with his birds and also on the estate I left. Please remember me kindly to Miss Florence and Miss Sybil, hoping her pains have left her. Thank you very much for sending my picture home I shall keep it as long as I live. They will not let me get up only half day so I have not seen inside the Chapel yet but hope to before long. We are not getting many cricket matches now as the weather is so bad, but they are very amusing to watch.

P.S. I suppose you will have patients from London Hospitals.

David Bogg, Bowers House, Nateby, near Garstang, Lancs, undated:
I suppose Miss Margaret [perhaps Margaret Amherst, another of the daughters of Lord Amherst] has informed you that I have got my discharge from the Army, and am in my old

place again, but not very comfortable. I suppose you have heard news of my dear brother being killed in action.

I am getting treated awfully bad up here. How is your chickens doing, hope splendidly. If I could only afford it I would come and look after them for you … but you see I am only getting 12/6 from the Army, if you want anyone to help you I will come willingly. Providing I can get just enough for my keep. So if you really want any assistance let me know as soon as possible, should love to come and help you.

Hoping her Ladyship and Miss Syball [sic] are quite well.

Florence's address book reveals that Bogg was the son of a former gamekeeper at Didilngton, so presumably he felt that he could ask for work on the estate: Florence wrote back, not offering him work but promising she 'would try and find him a Poultry place'.

From Concerned Parents

From Mrs Emma Kirk, 60 Trafford St, Scunthorpe:
Dear Madam, Thank you very much for you writing to me, I was pleased to hear from you, yes I am glad to say I feel a little better but still I feel upset after the Air Raid that we had at Scunthorpe. I have never been the same since. I am glad to hear that my son is getting better again but he is still without his voice. It seems a long time coming back to him. I know it is a long journey for him and very bad weather. I know he longs to see him [sic, means 'me'] and I should like to see him. Will you tell him to rest contented and not to worry over me. Thank you very much for taking such great care of him, as it is a load off my mind, and I am also glad to hear he is so happy and has every attention. Trusting he will rest alright as I am always worrying over him.

P.S. You see it is 12 months since I saw him.

From Mrs Emma Kirk:
Dear Madam, in answer to your letter which I received with many thanks. I was very glad to hear from you and also pleased to hear that my son is on the improve, as it has worried me to think that he has suffered so much and not able to go and see him. You see it would be such an expense to me but still I am longing to see my son. I think if I could only see him I should feel much better as I often sit down and have a good cry over him. I think he must have suffered a lot. Has he had an operation as you do not state what they have done to him, but as long as he can speak I can rest contented, as it is an anxious time for us all. Thank you very much for taking so much interest in him, as it is a load off my mind to think he can do same as myself and that is to speak. I should very much like to see him. Do you think they will be long before they let him return home now he has received it. I wish you to thank Sister Ethel very much for my kindness towards my son, I would write to her if I knew her name and address. Trusting to hear again from you in the meantime as I would like to know if it will be successful.

From a Former Nurse

Doris E. Briscoe, Nethercourt Auxiliary Military Hospital, Ramsgate, 1 May [no year]:

My dear 'Matron',

I have not been able to write to you before as I did not know whereabouts I was being sent. I arrived here on Friday and went on night duty – for two months night duty seems to be my fate. This is a very large hospital – for acute cases only. The cases come direct from the hospital ships and in many cases the men have only been wounded 12 hours previously. This speaks well for our transportation doesn't it!

The men are housed in large wooden huts. 75 beds in each hut. There are some dreadful cases among them. I go on duty from 9 pm to 9 am and I can assure you I get very little time to sit down. Of course I have several VAD's and two RAMC orderlies on with me – but the responsibility is a very big one as you can imagine.

However I am very glad to be here as the work is splendid and I can almost fancy I am back in France again. We have Zeppelin scares practically every night – all this adds to the excitement of night duty.

I saw the three boys at Eastbourne on Easter Monday – they were not too happy I fancy. Sergeant Robinson was alright because he had no work to do but the others had spent the whole morning scrubbing floors which they did not at all like after Buckenham. However I guess they will get used to it in time and it will help to harden them for a soldier's life again.

I expect you are feeling pretty strange without your hospital work but I am sure you need a good long rest. I hope your sister is feeling better and that her knees are not worrying her much. Please give her my kind regards. I do not know your address so I hoping that this will find you.

Very few records have survived of auxiliary hospitals. These letters give fascinating details of soldiers' and nurses' lives in Norfolk in the First World War.

5

THE HOME FRONT

Norfolk people did not need to go abroad to take part in the war: the war came to Norfolk. The first ever air raid on Britain in which lives were lost took place over Yarmouth and King's Lynn in January 1915. There was a Zeppelin raid on East Dereham in September 1915.

Fifty years later, two sisters, Ethel and Gertrude Weir (later Ethel Neeve and Gertrude Ayton), remembered the events. At the time of the raid, Gertrude was fifteen and Ethel just eleven years old. The family dived into their cellar when they heard the droning of the airship.

Ethel recalled: 'We heard it coming over. My father said, "Don't make a noise. Keep still." It went right over the garden. Dad said we could go up, so we all came out and saw it ever so plainly.'

She described the cigar-shaped gasbag with the cabin slung underneath as 'a great long thing making a tremendous noise'. It flew very low over the house and dropped a bomb which failed to explode – in the meadow at the back. 'If they had dropped that bomb a bit sooner it would have landed on us,' she continued. Gertrude added, 'I don't think we were frightened. We were so excited to see it.'

Another child witness was Jennie Fitt (later Jennie McDonagh), daughter of the town curate; she was ten years old at the time of the raid. In later life, she recalled,

A small bomb fell, hitting the coping of the Dereham church tower and burying itself in the ground at the foot. But it did not explode. That 'curtain-raiser' was followed by loud explosions that shook window frames and made walls shudder. The sound of explosions continued for some time.

'It is a Zeppelin raid', my father said, in a quiet voice. 'We must all go into the kitchen and sit near the middle wall'. My mother and sister, aged 14, and my brother who was 13, and our little maid, and, of course myself, all sat closely together in the darkness, all very frightened. But no-one cried. I covered my ears with my hands and tried to shut out the sound of the bombs exploding. After what seemed a long while, there was a lull, then silence. No more bombs fell. My father said, 'I am going outside to see what is happening'. My sister at once got up and followed him, as she was deeply attached to her father. Very soon they returned, and he said, 'it is not over yet'. Later my father told us he had looked up and seen the grey pencil-shaped Zeppelin, silhouetted against the sky, appearing to be drifting with its engines shut off.

Hardly had my father returned inside the house, than bombs started falling again. The explosions seemed to fill the house, dying away and ending in a dull exhausted thud. Suddenly, we heard a different sound, like gunfire, but we had no anti-aircraft guns in the town. Then, soon after, there was a long silence, and no more bombs fell. My mother got up and said she was going to make some tea, our little maid following her. As my mother waited for the kettle to boil, she ran upstairs to the landing window and looked across the town. Running down, she said, 'It looks as if the town is on fire'. Her voice trembled. 'Drink your tea, children,' she said, 'It's safe to go to bed now. Lie on your bed in your clothes'. And my father said, 'The raid is over. The Zeppelins have gone. If you go to sleep we will go out early and see what has happened in the town'.

About five o'clock in the morning our mother called us to come down quickly for some bread and butter and hot tea, then we set off with father to look at our town. In less than half a mile we reached the centre. Church Street was a shambles. The entire glass roof of the Corn Hall was gone. The shops and houses on either side were badly damaged and their contents strewn across the road, all sorts of things lying among the brick and glass and rubble.

'Keep in the middle of the road. Please,' instructed Police Constable Brown, as he stood in the ruins of Church Street. The walls left standing were pocked with shrapnel holes and the interiors of small houses exposed to gaze. We walked on beyond the church to some fields where a number of bombs had fallen. There were huge craters, big enough to hide a small modern car. We found many pieces of shrapnel in the mud, and my father caught his foot in a piece of iron handle. One or two large bombs that had not exploded were about the height of a small girl. In fact, the farmer in whose fields the bombs had fallen had his two little girls, one five and the other six, photographed by our local photographer standing one each side of the bomb. The bomb was painted khaki and pear-shaped, with an iron casing on top, and iron handles.

We learned on our way home that four people had been killed and four injured in the night's raid. The sound of the maroons [loud fireworks used as a signal] set off to call the fire brigade to come and quench a fire in the paint stores of the ironmongers' shop must have been interpreted by those commanding the Zeppelins as anti-aircraft fire. So the enemy had fled to the coast for Germany. The raid was over. The bubbling sound of the engines faded in the distance.

A later report summarised what had happened:

[Damage] was confined apparently to a small area around the Market Place, Church Street, Withburga Lane and the Market Place itself. In Norwich Street, High Street and Commercial Road little damage was done, but over most of the rest of the town windows were shattered by the exploding bombs. Telegraph poles were knocked down cutting communications for several hours. Eight or nine bombs fell in the grounds of the Vicarage, which was being used by the Red Cross. Some fell near the hospital and the soldier patients, all convalescing, ran out in

Pulham Air Base:
the men who
flew the airships
and the women
who fought the
fires. The airships
were known as
'Pulham Pigs'. (MC
2254/183)

Norwich Market
Place. (Courtesy of
Michael Jordan)

pyjamas and nightshirts to smother fires with their blankets. At the Vicarage the biggest bomb crater was 23 yards round and over five feet deep and an unexploded bomb which was dug up was a few pounds short of a hundredweight.

The report, after detailing damage, says it is impossible to give a complete list and estimates that over 130 houses 'were more or less knocked about'. It was the same with injuries. Apart from the dead, it was impossible to say how many people had received serious or minor injuries. The report continues:

It was usual in those days to summon the fire brigade by maroons and immediately after fires had broken out Mr Herbert Leech ran to the King's Arms, where the maroons were kept, 'with a view of requesting the alarm to be fired'. But the unlucky Mr Leech 'found all the occupants down the cellars'. No one, apparently would run the risk of firing the maroons with bombs dropping all over the place. So Mr Leech got the key to the house where the maroons were kept and got the bombs out with the assistance of a soldier who had been passing.

Although he knew nothing about the firing of them, he (Mr Leech) made the attempt, actually holding the match in his hand whilst lighting the fuse. When the first maroon was fired the soldier rolled over amongst the cabbages in the garden and then bolted, but nothing daunted, Mr Leech fired a second bomb, at great personal risk, as the Zeppelin was then hanging overhead. Immediately after the maroons were fired, the Zeppelin fled and many attributed its departure to Mr Leech's pluck. For this he was complimented by the military officers and other prominent personages.

Those killed were James Taylor, who kept an earthenware shop in the High Street, Harry Patterson, a jeweller, and soldiers of the City of London Yeomanry.

As Edith Upcher's diary showed, invasion was a real threat. Official preparations were made:

Possible German Landing; Instructions to Emergency Special Constables:
In the event of a landing, an instruction will be sent to the special constables either TO PREPARE or TO ACT at once.

TO PREPARE will mean that the special constables give notice to the inhabitants to make preparations in case they have to leave the district. These preparations will consist in getting together horses, mules and donkeys, and any things that they can move in their carts.

TO ACT at once will mean that Special Constables are requested to inform the inhabitants, who wish to leave that they are to get out of the district as quickly as possible with their horses and carts, that they are to destroy all petrol, spades, picks, saws and axes, that they are to render useless or destroy carts, blacksmiths' forges, and by removing some of the machinery to render corn mills and traction engines useless, but not to burn the mills. The Special Constables are to arrange to leave no horses, cattle or sheep for the use of the enemy. The inhabitants must on no account travel to NORWICH and main roads should be avoided.

People are advised to make their way by bye-roads to the South-West where possible, but which route is taken must depend upon the direction of the enemy advance, and the best advice will be given at the time.

Stock, stacks, buildings and other property are only to be destroyed by order of the Military and receipt forms will be provided for use in case of the destruction of property by order of the Military Authorities.

All owners of stock are recommended to mark their stock with the letter 'B' to denote their district and also with their private mark, and to register the latter with the police to facilitate compensation claims.

Should the order be given to destroy cattle the Committee are advised the following method will probably be best: the cattle to be driven into boxes or small enclosures as close as they can be packed so that there is no room for any of them to move. The stock should then be shot behind or near the ear with an ordinary shot gun held at a short distance.

As this shows, Norfolk was a farming county. As the German blockade began to bite, the production of food became a vital issue: all possible spaces were utilised. Using men for the harvest was at least as important as using them in battle. In June 1917, the War Office agreed not to take any more men employed on farms without the consent of that county's Agricultural Executive Committee.

When conscription was introduced in 1916, men who thought they had a case for not being sent to war could go through tribunals and put their case. A small number of people refused to fight on religious or moral grounds – the well-known conscientious objector – but local newspapers show that most people who came before these tribunals were claiming exemption not on principle, but on the grounds that they were doing vital work at home. Each case was considered individually, as those considered on one random day in 1917 show:

On the farm. (MC 2283/1)

Holt Post, 22 June 1917
Norfolk Appeal Tribunal

Six agricultural cases down for hearing were referred to the Norfolk War Executive Committee.

The case of a Yarmouth carpenter, whose case had been adjourned for two months, came up again before the Tribunal. It appeared that he was not only a carpenter, but in the evenings he played the drum in the band of a picture palace.

The Chairman: We can't keep a man to beat the big drum.

The Tribunal were informed that he was a C1 man with a wife and a family of six children, of whom all but one are dependent on him, and that during the daytime he was engaged in making ammunition boxes.

Mr Costello said carpenters would be needed in the Army; but the Tribunal granted conditional exemption.

Yarmouth Tribunal

A naval and military tailor, aged 41, single and class A, was ordered to serve at the end of a month. He had nearly £600 worth of stock, and that it was very hard lines having to throw up his business after he had taken so many years to build it up.

A married man, aged 37, in business as a coal hawker and general carrier, said he had been in business for nearly seven years and traded in the poorer parts of the town. He had had ten children, of whom seven survived, not one of whom earned enough to keep herself. The last daughter was born on Good Friday. He was in the Volunteers. Three month's temporary [postponement of call up].

Aged 18, the driver of a 30 ft motor fishing boat, was appealed for on the ground that such workmen were very scarce and fish are wanted for food. His father was skipper of the boat. Six months' temporary.

Many men were too old to be called up, and watched the war from home. One such man was Henry Rider Haggard, the author of best-selling books like *King Solomon's Mines* and *She*. He kept a diary recording local and national events:

1 September 1914:
I came to London on Saturday Aug 29 and thence home [Ditchingham] where I found all well and the harvest up. The station at Liverpool Street was full of soldiers sitting about on their kitbags. The first news that greeted us here was the glad tidings of the brilliant and successful naval action of Heliogoland. Would that more of the Germans had come out. With it were rumours that all is not well so far as our expeditionary force in Belgium was concerned. Their retreat seemed to be continuous but the facts are hidden. London seemed much as usual. On Monday I returned to Town from Ditchingham which appeared as peaceful as though war were a word unknown, to see my chairman Lord d'Abernon as to Commission affairs. He had made an appointment for me with Mr Harcourt whom I saw at the House of Commons at 4 o'clock ... He seemed of the opinion that the war could last a long time, perhaps two or three years. He denied the

On the farm. (ACC 2013/320)

On the farm. (MC 2283/1)

rumours as to Russian troops passing through England with energy and in detail, but whether he did this to blind me I cannot say. Certainly those rumours are most persistent. Mr Harcourt said that they arose from the journey of Scotch Gaelic-speaking regiments. He took a hopeful view of matters, alleging that there had been no disaster, though the French had missed some great opportunity, presumably by their excursion into Alsace. It seems that French has reported the casualties at only about 5,000, which, he declared, astonished him, as it did me …

Today (1 Sep) I saw Charles Longman as to writing a history of the war if we should all live so long. He said nothing could be sold and no money collected and it was difficult to know how to meet outgoings. Also his boy Freddie is somewhere at the front and he knows not what is happening to him. Charles Graves whom I saw at the Club is in like anxiety about his son and looks wretched. But there, we are all in the same boat. Both Mark and George [nephews of Haggard] are in Belgium, the first fighting in the Welch regiment, the second trapped as a civilian. Mark, I hear, announced that he would never live to be taken prisoner. His poor young bride is in a sad state of anxiety … At lunch at the Club I sat next to Birrell the Irish Secretary and had a long talk with him. He was in low spirits and thought things most serious. Our losses up to date he put at 15,000, a different total to French's 5,000. He wondered whether the Russians would remain faithful to their allies or be 'bought off', a cheerful suggestion truly!

2 September 1914:
No more news or certainly none that is good. First list of casualties, but few names. About 4,000 missing, which I suppose means in most cases dead, as the Germans do not seem to take many prisoners. Probably these poor fellows were left behind in the retreat. I forgot to say that Harcourt told me that about 80,000 Indian troops would land at Marseilles in a few days. I wish there were 800,000 of them!

9 September:
During the past week there has been little definite news, but continual rumours as to Russian troops passing through England, so continual that I begin to think Harcourt must have lied to me – or been in the dark himself. On Thursday officers arrived here. We have put up three, Major Verden, Captain de Koop and Lt Wilson of the Cheshire Yeomanry. The whole district is full of soldiers. We are to have artillery camped on one field near Mann's Maltings. The Cheshires are by the other Maltings but are being moved because of the damp mist at night. Poor people! There have been sent here without blankets, tents or even greatcoats and have to walk about at nigh to keep themselves warm. Thus do we prepare our volunteer forces for service.

On Friday after returning from seeing the Wills at Bradenham I attended a recruiting meeting in Bungay. My speech was well received to put it mildly, and I am glad to say that then and after the meeting we got 75 recruits. This was good for a little town whence many had already gone as Territorials etc.

18 September:
I have just heard over the telephone from my daughter Angie that her brother-in-law, and my nephew, Mark Haggard 'died of wounds' on the 15th. It was a great shock. He was a good officer (Welch Regiment) and a very gallant man. As I have mentioned, his mother told me only the other day – or perhaps it was Tom – that he said before he left that never would he live to be taken prisoner by the Germans. Well, he has not lived. All honour to him who has died the best and greatest of deaths. The first to go of the 6 or 7 I have concerned. I write this at the dining table where so often he has sat and almost it seems to me he answers my toast to him from the Valhalla whither he has passed. But his poor young wife whose marriage I attended not a year ago! R. I. P.

The Russian business, I mean as to passage of 10,000 of them through England has been finally exploded. So Harcourt did not lie to me after all. It is the most extraordinary instance of a national hallucination that I have met in the course of my life. Everyone I know seems to have seen these Russians. I suppose that it arises from keeping the public in the dark.

25 September:
No more news. The siege goes on, that is all. Louie met the recruiting officer today who tells her the men are no longer coming in fast in Norfolk. The keen one have joined and others do not wish to join. Also the women are the great obstacle. Hundreds of them refuse to allow their sons to go. In that class of life women as a body seem to lack patriotic spirit, which is a great argument against giving them the vote. Nor is this evil attitude entirely confined to villagers and trades folk as I happen to know. As I wrote to Lord Roberts today I believe it must come to conscription at last – the sooner the better as I think …

I have heard more details of Mark's death supplied to his mother by an officer of his regiment, Lieut. Somerset who was in the next bed to him in the hospital. It seems that he got ahead of his men and killed the three German gunners serving the gun he was charging with his own hand, then was struck down. He died quite suddenly about 36 hours afterwards just as he was talking. No doubt some internal haemorrhage. He told them he was so glad to find he was not 'afraid' when the moment came. Mark 'afraid'!

16 January 1915:

In one of the letters from the front published in *The Times* and written by a cavalry officer, its author makes a remark which has struck me. Speaking of the absence of his C. O. who has been killed, he says that what strikes him most is 'the fact that no-one speaks of the dead. It is just as though he had never existed … and the loss could never be emphasised by words as much as it is by the dead silence in that regard. The last day or two we brightened up a bit in the Mess but never a word about those that are missing'. This is very interesting but after all only an exemplification of the common instinct upon a rather more extended scale than usual. Nobody does like talking of the dead except – well, except some who do, generally women. In the fact of death, unless we are very shallow, or very deep indeed, most of us find ourselves face to face with something too tremendous to accommodate itself to casual conversation. The dead who a few minutes ago was laughing and joking in a trench, the most commonplace of mortals, or trudging his daily round in civilian life, what is he now? Nothing or everything – which? In the midst of all the shams and unrealities of what is called civilised life, that is, life lived in a web of conventions where escape from the truth is the most desirable of aims, this black ugly head of death thrusts up and will not be escaped. No wonder that the butterflies do not care to spread their wings upon it. In some ways I think the war is doing good in England. It is bringing the people, or some of them, face to face with elementary facts which hitherto it has been the fashion to ignore and pretend are non-existent. To take one every humble example. How often have I been vituperated by rose-water critics because I have written of fighting and tried to inculcate certain elementary lessons such as that it is a man's duty to defend his country, and that only those who are prepared for war can protect themselves and such as are dear to them. 'Coarse! – bloody! brutal! uncivilised!' – such has been the talk. Well, and today have I done any harm by inculcating a certain number of the thousands who are at the front with these primary facts, even though my work has been held to be so infinitely inferior to that of Oscar Wilde, Bernard Shaw and others? The worst of it is that here in England we have not as yet half learned the lesson, nor will it ever be learned unless the nation is forced through a straight and narrow gate of misery that I hope and pray it will never be called upon to pass.

20 January 1915:

Today there really is a piece of news. The Zeppelins have visited my native shores and dropped bombs on Yarmouth, Lynn, Sandringham and sundry other places, killing a number of innocent people and frightening a great many more. The Government issues no statement whatever and the Public is left to pick up information as best it can. There is a rumour that one of the Zeppelins was shot down by a man-of-war off the coast, but this is probably much too good to be true. The expedition can have served no military purpose whatsoever and is merely another example of German wickedness played off upon a nation which they know will not retaliate in kind. May the deed lie heavy on their souls in this world and every other. I suppose that the raid was a mere trial trip before attacking London.

Many soldiers from all over Britain came to Norfolk for training. Many acres of the county were taken up, including the grounds of some of the great halls like Sheringham. H. M. Upcher, the Hall's owner, wrote to 'Sir Forrest' on 9 December 1914:

We are simply a Military camp. We have seven officers and 60 men sleeping in the house. Every barn and granary is full of men and every conceivable corner of horses. The Park begins to look like a ploughed field. Half the fields dug up with trenches and one cannot call anything one's own. However, better them than the Germans – Yes indeed the peace seeking Government has much to answer for. No men, no rifles and the immense sacrifice of life caused by their unpreparedness. It would indeed be a relief to know the German fleet was badly crippled.

Air raids led to anti-German feelings, which were made worse after the *Lusitania* was sunk with the loss of many innocent lives. Windows were smashed in shops whose owners had German-sounding names. Joyce Carr saw this in London:

15 May 1915:
Yesterday when I was in Southwark and Walworth, I saw a great many remains of those horrible riots. Every German shop was shut up and guarded by policemen. As almost every baker in those regions and east London was German, I cannot think what they will do for bread. However, it's their own look out.

Taking a break from training on the Norfolk coast. (MC 2883/1)

Map reading 'under fire'. (MC 2283/1)

6

FRANK DUNHAM'S WAR

One of the most complete diaries left by a Norfolk soldier is the war diary of Frank H. Dunham of Meadow Rise Road, Norwich. After the war, he edited this for publication, but it has never in fact been published: we have only space here for extracts from some of the earlier entries:

Frank Dunham. (MC 947/1)

10 April 1916:

Having been passed A.1. at Britannia Barracks, Norwich I obtained permission to join the Cyclists Battn, The 25th London Regt, and was given a free railway pass to London, where I had to report their H.Q's at Putney. Falling back on the old excuse of 'to wind up business affairs', I managed to get 5 days leave at once, and by that time got used to wearing khaki. Returning to Putney, we spent a few days drilling at H.Q's and were then sent to join the 3rd Battn at Feltham, Middlesex. We were billeted with civilians, and I was comfortably fixed up with Mrs Wakeley at 9 Victoria Road, sharing a bed with a corporal, who had already been there some weeks … I was in early trouble with the military police, for walking out one evening with the collar hook of the great coat undone, and it appeared that they delighted in exercising their authority on a 'rookie'. Gun training consisted chiefly of early morning physical training, drill and rank marches, for although we were in a Cyclists Battn, there was never any issue of cycles to us.

Many rumours were in the air as to our going under canvas, and eventually on May 2nd we marched in the pouring rain to Richmond Park, where we were received with much cheering from the H.A.C. and the London Scottish, who were already encamped there. We spent an uncomfortable night, 14 wet 'Tommies' in a bell tent, but we soon settled down to this new life and the weather improving, we had some real good times. The approach of winter was the sign for troops to be moved into hutted camps, and our turn came on September [word crossed out] 14th, when the Battn moved to Fovant Camp, Salisbury Plain. Actually around Fovant, (a small village), there were numerous camps, and ours was called Hurdcott Camp. Our move here was not at all to our liking, and it proved to be a very dull place for us, after Richmond Park. Gun training became much stricter, and bayonet fighting over a prepared course became almost a daily occurrence.

On October 18th a draft of 300 men was selected, myself included, for service overseas, but our destination was not made known to us, and on the 20th we were granted 48 hours leave and threatened with severe punishment if we did not return to time. On returning from leave, we spent one day landing the surplus kit etc, and the next day, Tuesday October 24th, saw us entrain at Salisbury at 2 p.m. en route for Southampton. By 5 p.m. with drafts from other battalions, we were on board the 'Moona Queen' and then followed 9 hours of unpleasantness, for myself at any rate, as it was a rough sea, and we eventually reached Havre at 2 a.m, although we did not land until 7 a.m. We marched straight away to Harfleur Camp, situated just outside Havre, and it was an eye opener to us to see the enormous ammunition dumps etc. En-route, we were pestered with children begging for 'souvenir biscuits', (it seemed as if they were very keen on our army biscuits) and old girls selling bottles of beer and wine. We had received orders that none of the latter were to be brought, nevertheless, several found their way into the ranks, but from remarks passed, it appeared to be poor stuff.

We found Harfleur Camp to be a huge affair, consisting of many small camps, all numbered, and we were put into No 15 Camp. All were under canvas, and as far as the eye could see appeared to be bell tents. Whilst we had about 10 in each tent, the officers were far more comfortable, by having a small canvas hut between two large marquees served as mess rooms, whilst there were also several Y.M.C.A and Church Army tents, in which one could buy refreshments and play games. It was here that I first saw the only gambling game allowed in the army – the famous game of 'House' – of course, many other games went on, such as, 'brown and anchor', 'Pontoon' etc, and these the authorities had to shut their eyes to. Training, much different from that we had received in England, proceeded rapidly, and each morning we paraded, we were issued with dinner rations, and marched up a very steep hill to a plain, called the 'Bull Ring', where we received expert instructions in the art of warfare. All the instructions were either officers or sergts with actual fighting experiences, and through wearing yellow bands on their arms, were known to the troops as the 'Canaries'. We soon found that there were seven working days in the week over this side, for on Sundays we were marched to the docks at Havre, and had to spend 6 hours unloading ships …

We had some local excitement, when one of the chaps in our tent was a suspected case of the measles, and consequently our tent was isolated, and we were not allowed out. This suited us all right, no work to do, and meals brought to our door. From memory, I should say we averaged 16 hours sleep each day, and work came very hard to us again when we were released in 7 days' time.

Just previous to being put on draft we were transformed to the 3/10 London Regt by name only, but on arriving at Havre we were paraded and ordered to hand over our 25th London badges, and in return received the badge of the 7th London Regt. This Regt had earned for itself the name of the 'Shiny Seventh', by being one of the first to commence cleaning their buttons etc on active service, and we were not overjoyed at the prospect of joining them, as we had dumped all our cleaning kit before leaving England, and anticipated having finished with this job. November arriving, the weather turned very cold, and we had snow on more than one occasion, and this usually turned some of the roads into floating seas of mud. We were served out with service rifles and bayonets, all of which had been in use before, and my bayonet had some blood stains on it, which, you can imagine I soon obliterated. The latest type of box respirator followed, and these we had to test in gas chambers at the 'Bull Ring' – when in danger zones, these could be worn on the chest, nice and handy in the 'alert' position.

As a wind up to our training, we had a few lectures on actual incidents at the front, but from what we saw later, found that they had been very highly coloured. November 16th at 8pm found us parading for the last time in Camp 15, and marching to Harfleur Halte, we entrained in cattle trucks at midnight. It seemed curious to notice all the trucks marked 'Hommes 40, Cheveaux 8', and really how 40 of us packed ourselves into one truck I hardly know, for our kit took up plenty of room. Several chaps found nails, and knocked them into the sides of the truck, to hang their equipment up, but the jolting of the train brought several of them down, which was the means of releasing a sudden flow of delicate language from the unfortunate individual who had stopped their descent. We travelled at a very slow pace, and had numerous stops, but we soon picked up the dodge of getting hot water from the engine driver, to make tea with.

Nobody appeared to know where we were bound for, but eventually at 8 a.m, on the 17th, we arrived at Rouen, and disembarked. We were right glad to stretch our legs, and all went into a large coffee hut where we rested until 3 p.m. At 5 pm. we entrained again, and from this time, were 28 hours before we reached our destination. It seemed a terrible long time to us, and getting so tired and stiff, we laid all over each other in the truck, and got [word crossed out] accustomed to finding a nice army boot resting on our heads. However, all things come to an end, and in pitch black at 9 pm. on November 18th, we noticed the train stop, and then heard orders to alight. We found that we were at Abeele, and had travelled via Boulogne, Calais and Hazebrouck. A pleasant cold steady rain was falling, and off we marched to a reinforcement camp under canvas nearby. Apparently we were not expected, for no preparations were made for us, but the only thing we needed was a comfortable sleep, and with 16 in a tent we helped to keep each other warm. During the night we could hear the sound of guns firing in the distance, and in the morning, ascertained that we were at the rear of the Ypres area, and that our battalion, the 1/7th London Regt, was at the moment out of the line resting. We stayed in this camp until November 20th, and by this time had got somewhat used to rough camp conditions. Leaving at 7.30 a.m. our draft marched towards the line, and eventually found the 7th London in a camp of wooden huts, called Halifax Camp – in time we found that all the camps in this area had been named by the Canadians, who had been here some time previously. This camp consisted of two rows of huts running by the roadside for a distance of about 200 yards, and was situated on the right of the road between Ouderdom and Vlamertinghe.

It was here that we saw our first real signs of war, and except for khaki, the whole place appeared deserted, and houses etc could be seen which had suffered from shell fire. We were received in camp by Lt Col. C.J.S. Green, who gave us a lecture on our duties etc, and then asked for specialists, i.e, men who had received special training in any branch of infantry work. Running over the list he called out, 'Stretcher Bearers', and I having obtained my first aid certificate with the British Red Cross Society in 1915, fell out, with three others, Michell, Hitchcock and Brown, by name. Up till this time, I was of opinion, that the R.A.M.C. were responsible for all wounded, but I now discovered that each infantry battalion had four S.B's to each company, who were responsible for the sick and wounded, and had to take them to the Regimental Aid Post, from where they were evacuated by the R.A.M.C. We four were taken before the N.C.O in charge of S.B's, Corporal W. Leary, who questioned us, and then put one of us into each company, I being allotted to 'A'. We found all the battalion S.B's billeted together in one hut, and on entering, were soon introduced all round, and put at ease. My three company mates turned out to be Charles Phillips, who went overseas with the Division in March 1915, a Londoner born and bred, Edward Hone and 'Toby' Martin, both of Cobham, Surrey, who had enlisted with the East Surreys, and been sent out on draft to the 7th London in September 1916 …

I soon found out that the S.Bs usually did duty in pairs and Hone and Martin being pals, I consequently went with Phillips. Most of the section by now being 'old soldiers', we four new comers heard plenty of yarns about the front line etc, but the battalion having only recently left the severe fighting on the Somme, meant that all of them had seen something, and they were part of the fortunate 92, who came [word crossed out] from these battles untouched, out of a battalion strength of 600. During the day, I had issued to me a S.B armlet, and I in turn, handed over my rifle to C.S.M Childs of 'A' Coy …

A blanket per man was issue for sleeping, and Phillips and I found it beneficial to sleep together, and share our blankets and great coats. This night was uneventful, but on wishing to wash the next morning, found that the only water obtainable was that in the ditches and shell holes near the camp – my mess-tin had to serve as my shaving mug, and I even noticed some chaps shaving with their last drop of hot tea rather than shaving in cold water. Our food rations were good, and what surprised me was the amount of cheese that was wasted. All rations with the exception of meat, bacon, tea + sugar were issued direct to us, bread usually working out at a 2lb loaf between three men per day. By this time the rat-tat of machine guns could be plainly heard, and several bullets fell around us – I instinctively ducked, but Phillips laughed, and asked me if I wanted one in my head as they were dropping at our feet, nevertheless, the first sensation of hearing bullets whistle around you is a strange one. After walking for about another 20 minutes, we came upon a trench full of the troops we were to relieve, who soon got out of it, and we jumped down, and found the S.Bs dugout to be built in the side of the trench and only 2 feet high. This meant that we could just crawl into it and lie down – we soon had a candle alight, but had to make sure that the sack over the entrance did not let the light out. I passed a remark that we had not seen any shelling getting into the line, and the 'old sweats' told me that it seemed a mutual arrangement between Fritz and ourselves, not to shell whilst rations limbers and reliefs were about.

We found ourselves in the support line, being about 100 yards in rear of the front line, which half of our company was holding. This sector was to the S.E of Ypres, and known as the Ravine, and the trenches appeared in good condition. My first night in the trenches proved uneventful, and I slept well in spite of cold feet – we heard the next morning that the company men had been working during the night building up the sides of the communication trench and front line, which had been knocked about by shells recently. Owing to the mud in the trenches, we were all issued with rubber waders, and if these got wet through, we could change them for a further pair at a drying room, i.e a good sized dugout fitted with racks in which large braziers were kept going. In company orders appeared the notice that it was a crime to get 'trench feet', and everyone was expected to rub his feet daily with whale oil and have clean dry socks to change into. About 2 pm on November 24th, I had my first experience of shell fire, Fritz commenced sending over light shells and trench mortars, and continued this for 3 hours.

We sat in our dugout, which was just about splinter proof, and could hear several 'lumps' quite near us, and quite expected to be called out any minute to attend to casualties. However as it was getting dusk the shelling died down, and we were just congratulating ourselves on having no work to do when the call of 'Stretcher Bearers' floated up the trench. Out we got, and were told that 3 chaps had been hit by a shell which burst in the front line, and running up the communication trench found two, Austin and Wheeler, with slight wounds, which they had bandaged themselves with their field dressings and the other, Chambers, moaning in the bottom of the trench. Being dark by now, we couldn't see where he had been hit and he appeared in such pain, that we put him on the stretcher, and made off at once down the communication trench, and we had to climb on top of the trench and go through part of the Ravine Wood. I shall never forget this carry – it was slow work, and the mud in the wood was knee deep, we were slipping all over the place with the stretcher, and I felt sorry for poor old Chambers, who gave an extra loud moan every time the stretcher bumped. We four S.Bs were all done in by the time we reached the Aid Post, and we rested here a short time, while the M. C. saw after Chambers – he had an ugly looking wound in the small of the back. Cpl Leary was good enough to give us a mug of tea each, and thus refreshed, we returned to our dugout.

The next day, November 26th, whilst a small party was carrying stores from Jackson's Dump to the front line, two of them, Priddis and Greedy, were wounded slightly. Things remained fairly quiet in the line, and I was fast settling down to the general routine. In the support line where we were, our coy cooks had a dugout in which they made our tea and stew - they used charcoal as fuel, for it gave off no smoke. We had notice to be ready for relief on the evening of November 28th, and at 9pm, we handed over our dugout to the S.B's of the relieving battalion, and the company falling in single file, we went off back towards Ypres, all thoroughly glad that our first experience of trench life was over. All was quiet, mud, water and shell holes being our worst enemies, and it was so pitch black that our progress was very slow, and it was only by having the word passed back, that we knew when to step over a shell hole etc. Just outside Ypres, to our surprise, we entrained, and proceeded back through Vlamertinghe at a slow pace.

No smoking was allowed until we were well away from Ypres, and it was curious to see the cab of the engine covered in, to prevent any light escaping. The train pulling up, we alighted, not on to a platform, but into about 18" of mud – apparently nobody knew which way we had to go, but eventually we got on to a very cobbled road, and thence across fields. I think nearly all our chaps stumbled and fell during this march, as we were all tired out, but at last we saw the lights in the camp, and were shown into huts. This was about 3.30 a.m., all felt 'whacked to the wide', and it was all I could do to remove my mud-caked puttees and boots before I fell asleep.

The following day we had to ourselves, and we needed it too, what with cleaning up etc. I had a look round the camp, called Dominion Camp, which consisted of wooden huts, and duckboard tracks heading to each, and it appeared that we were in the midst of a mud flat, for to step off a duckboard meant going ankle deep in mud. The roofs of our huts rose from the ground at an angle of 45°, to about 9 ft high at the ridge, but contained no stoves whatever. The 'old soldiers' however had a blaze. By this time, I had learnt most of the 'wrinkles' of the S.B. section, who always had a hut on their own out of the line, and found that we very rarely went on parade, although it was unwise to be seen lounging about the camp whilst the battn was drilling etc, so our time was spent fairly evenly between Y.M.C.A huts and coffee houses. Quite in the centre of our camp here, was a small house in which a Belgian family sold coffee, sweets, cigarettes etc, and from the amount of money they handled from the 'Tommies', I should think they were 'well off' when the war ended.

Our second night in camp, Phillips, my bed partner, returned to the hut after a visit to an estaminet, and was 'well oiled', and it didn't take long for him for fall asleep. In the early hours of the morning, I heard such a moaning by my side, and soon found myself receiving his beer etc all over me. I called him some nice names, and in future I slept by myself if there were any signs of his having too much. This camp was famous for its rats, which appeared to exist on our rations. I remember one night, being awakened by a rat running over my face, and could hear them sniffing away at a parcel of food I had received from home. They would scurry off when disturbed, but would return when everything was quiet again. On many occasions these rats ate part of the contents of my parcels. I tried hanging the parcels up on a nail from the roof, but always the same result, and it appeared that the rats climbed down the string to the parcel – it became usual for us all to sleep with our heads under our blankets after one chap had his nose bitten by a rat.

On December 1st, the battn marched in relays to Poperinghe for baths, which were fitted up in large marquees, and controlled by a staff of unfit men. It consisted of several sprays fixed to the roof, under which were large tubs. Undressing in an outer tent, we handed in at a wicket our dirty shirts, vest and pants, and received three 'checks' in exchange then two men under each spray, we had the joyful experience of 2 minutes under hot water, which suddenly turned to cold, so that we were glad to get back to our dressing room, change our 'checks' for clean underclothing and get dressed. Close by our camp, was a hut called the Vauxhall Y.M.C.A hut, where we spent several evenings at impromptu concerts and singsongs. I soon found that our reliefs were done on specified dates, and it appeared at present that each battn in the division did 5 days in front line positions, 5 days in support, and 10 days in reserve positions at some camp, so that is was no surprise to us, when we paraded for the line again on December 8th, this time to go to a new sector. Once again we passed through Ypres, and out by the Lille Gate, but instead of turning to the left at Shrapnel Corner as on our last trip to the line, we kept straight on, and passed Woodcote House, Bedford House, and Lankhof Farm, all well in ruins –

I found out later that the cellars of these places had all been supported with props, sandbags etc so that troops could shelter in them. All along this road on the side nearest the line was a screen of wire netting, threaded with green and brown pieces of canvas, these being erected to prevent Fritz seeing movement on the road in daylight.

At Lankhof Farm we left the road and turned to the left on to a duckboard track, which was much broken by shell fire, and soon found ourselves walking by the side of a canal bank. My S.B. pals had been up here before, and explained that we were going to take over the line to the right of where we were previously, the Ypres-Commines Canal being our right flank. Several spots along this bank had names such as, 'Windy Corner', 'Sniper's Post', etc, and I found them well named for the German position being on top of a ridge, they overlooked us, and could snipe at us with some amount of success, and there was no dallying around them. Some more ruins, Chester Farm, loomed up on our left, and a little further up the bank, we found it to be honeycombed with tunnels, all connected up by one long tunnel, which ran down the centre of the bank. We were Battn in support, and took over these tunnels from the 24th London Regt, not bad this, as one was safe from shell fire in them. This whole bank was called the Bluff, and the galleries inside were fitted up with wire netting beds, which proved quite comfortable for sleeping on. Although only a stone's throw from the front line, we had a canteen here, well stocked with cigarettes, chocolate, tinned fruits etc, so we could vary our rations. The central tunnel ran quite to the position of the front line, and terminated at the craters which had been mined and blown previously. The tunnels were barely 6 ft high, and many times did I crack my head on the roof, but fortunately my shrapnel helmet took off most of the blows.

No trenches were possible, and the troops had to lie ['lay' crossed out] out anywhere under cover in day time, and at night had to patrol round them, which meant many encounters with Fritz, also on the same job. Inside the craters, we had a few duckboard walks which were absolutely necessary, as I have seen chaps sink to their waists in the mud, and had to be pulled put. Being in these Bluff tunnels our Coy did not have to do any trench work, but had their full share of working parties, working by a different system of 6 hour shifts with Canadian tunnellers. Ypres had always been noted for mining activity, and we found things in full swing when we arrived — special mining coys had been formed, and did nothing else. Our chaps' duty was to carry sand bags full of earth from the mine to the surface, and empty them — this meant continually walking in water ankle deep, which continually oozed up in the tunnels, and necessitated pumps always at work, which were worked by gas engines. As a S.B. I had to take my turn in accompanying these working parties, in case of any casualties, but being exempt from this work, usually found some out of the way spot, and had a sleep, relying on one of the 'bhoys' to call me when they were departing.

Although we did not know it at the time, we were assisting in preparing some of the mines which were exploded on June 7th 1917. It was interesting to watch these miners digging away, and strutting up with planks of wood, they went along and where the width of the tunnel permitted, trolleys were used to wheel the soil away. Another strange thing, was that these tunnels were lighted by electric light worked from a dynamo. Of course, the Germans were mining too, and it was a fine game of skill, both sides trying to outdo the other. Instruments were used for listening purposes to detect mining activities by the enemy, and if a mine was suspected, our people endeavoured to be as quiet as possible; the miners wore sandbags round their feet, and actually did no digging — all their work was done by cutting and lifting. It was a very risky job, as these chaps never knew but what an enemy mine might be exploded in their rear, blocking their tunnel, which would mean suffocation, if they were not dug out in time. This sort of thing happened on December 11th, we being the aggressors. Our battalion was warned beforehand of this, and all troops had to 'stand to', in case Fritz retaliated with a raid. Our 'C' Coy was holding the craters at the time, and 'Toby' Martin and I were detailed to go up with this company, during this 'do' to assist their S.B's in case of many casualties. We didn't relish this very much, however at 6.30 p.m., our people blew a mine into a German gallery, and the Bluff rocked like a ship. Fritz promptly put over a barrage of shells in case we might be making an attack, and things were most unhealthy for a time. We heard later that our miners, immediately after the explosion, dug like fury into the German gallery, and captured some Jerry miners, who had been cut off by the explosion. Things quietened down after about an hour, and no casualties, so Toby and I crept into a tunnel shaft close by for a sleep.

At 1.a.m. we were called out to the craters, to a chap with a revolver wound in his calf – we found that this chap and his pal were on patrol on the lip of a crater, and got separated – on seeing each other again, one thought the other a German, and fired at him, consequently this wound. After we had bandaged the wound this wounded hero shook hands with his pal and thanked him, for giving him a 'blighty one'. This patrol business was a nerve trying experience, especially round about these craters – sometimes Fritz would get in them with a machine gun, and play havoc until he was bombed out. December 12th was a very cold day, on which we had a lot of snow, and the state of the craters became worse than ever. At 11 pm, Toby and I were called out to the craters again, following a salvo of German shells into them, and were pointed out a figure almost buried in the mud. Somehow, in the dark, we managed to get him out, but found he had been killed by one of the shells – then ensued 3 hours hard 'graft', carrying the body down to battn H.Qs. In the dark, progress is naturally slow, but keeping to a duckboard track, carrying a dead weight it is doubly so and we were thoroughly relieved when this job was over – this poor old chap was buried next day in a cemetery near B.H.Q. (Chester Farm Cemetery), which was Quite near to the front line, and our pioneers made the wooden cross for his grave.

On December 13th, our Coy left the Bluff tunnels, and relieved 'D' Coy who had been holding the craters, and to reach them, we went up 'Thames St' communication trench – this was in a terrible state, mud thigh deep, all of us were constantly getting stuck in it, and had to assist to pull each other out. Of course, we S.B's had our 'well beloved' stretchers to carry, and this was well cursed before we reached our destination. The state of this trench can be imagined, when it is known that it took 3 hours for our company to get along this trench, about 400 yards long. Dugouts were very scarce in the craters, and there appeared nowhere where we S.B's could get into, but we were going to be as comfortable as possible, so found ourselves a place in 'C' tunnel in the Bluff close by – we informed the Coy N.C.O's where our place was, so that we could be quickly found if needed. Part of our company was holding the front line to the left of the craters, and some in support trenches, names 'Pork + Bean' and 'King St'. The communication trench from 'King St' to the front line was called 'The Wynde' (all these trenches were marked by signboards), and ran parallel with the Bluff. This trench received plenty of attention from Fritz, and it was a very unhealthy quarter everyone getting through it as quietly as they could. Every night saw working parties busy repairing the damage done by shells, but the boggy nature of the soil made it difficult to keep the trench in good order. It also acted as a drain for part of the front line, consequently the rain together with so much shelling made a filthy mess of the trench. The whole area was so wet round about here that it used to be said 'that water must run uphill here'.

On December 14th, Fritz shelled our duckboard track connecting the tunnel entrances, very heavily the whole morning. I happened to be on the track (getting some fresh air as the tunnels were naturally stuffy) when he started, but quickly returned to our tunnel for safety. Later in the day, two dead Jerries were brought down to H.Q., having been taken from the craters. The next morning Fritz gave us another dose of shelling, and it proved to be an exceedingly heavy bombardment for about 2 hours, but it is surprising that only very few shells inflict damage, and our casualties from this were 1 killed and 3 wounded. In retaliation, our batteries commenced at 2 p.m. and kept up a heavy fire until 4 pm, but naturally we could not see what damage they were doing. On December 16th, Phillips and I relieved 'Buffo' and 'Toby', at 1 pm. We now found ourselves with our front line platoon, and we had an apology for a dug-out situated quite at the corner of The Wynde and the front line. This dugout had one layer of sand bags on top, resting on a sheet of corrugated iron, just enough to keep the rain out, but any small shell would easily penetrate it. It was only 6ft by 4ft, and 3ft high, just room for two of us, but somehow it had a charmed life, for we were in that self-same dug out several times later on, and it was still as sound as on this day. This was my first experience of being in the front line, and it produced a curious sensation to think the enemy were so near.

Some of the 'old stagers' endeavoured to put the 'wind up' we 'rookies', by suggesting that perhaps Fritz might make a night raid on our trench – this would mean that he would either kill or capture our sentries and give us a bomb in each dugout before he returned to his own trenches, however, no thoughts of such happenings kept me from sleeping soundly that night. The company men were not so fortunate, having to do 2 hours sentry duty and 4 hours off duty in their dugouts (if they had one – some had to sleep in the bottom of the trench with a ground-sheet over the top to keep them dry) right through the night – after dark, the sentries were always in pairs to prevent each other from falling asleep. The next morning, I had a walk down the front line trench, just to see what it was like, and being tall, I had to stoop well, so as not to provide a target for a Fritz sniper. This trench was a poor affair, in many places there was only a front to it composed of Breastwork of sandbags, as the nature of the soil would not allow a trench to be dug. A peep though a periscope proved interesting – I could see our and Jerries' barbed wire, also his front line trench in places, but no signs of a living thing. The top of the periscope has to protrude above the trench, and it was one of the sports of snipers to aim at smashing the opposing side's periscopes, although one had to be a jolly good shot to hit such a small target.

Quite near to our dugout the German trench ran in quite close to ours, and on still nights, we could hear Fritz walking on his duckboards and talking to his comrades. Being a sentry at night, was far from a pleasant job, as often, without warning a machine gun would play on the parapet, and it necessitated 'ducking' to prevent being hit. Also it was a strain on the eyes, trying to peer through the darkness – one night one of our chaps on sentry thought he saw a movement in front of him, and fired, and when the next verey light went up, he found that he had killed a large rat. For three afternoons running, Fritz served us up with a heavy trench mortar 'Straffe', we naturally retaliated, and this made things lively. Our pet names for Fritz's trench mortar shells, were 'Toffee-apples' and 'Rum jars', names after the shape of them – we could see them flung high in the air, and watch them come wobbling over in our direction. It was generally possible to dodge them, by darting away from where you thought the shell would drop, but if two came over together aimed at different spots, then it was difficult. I tried dodging them at first, as I knew our dugout was useless, if one landed on it, but I got tired of this, and went into the dugout with Phillips, and chanced my luck.

On the second afternoon, Phillips (he was a sly old dog) left me just before the shelling commenced as he wished to make some purchases from the canteen in the tunnels, and I was the only S.B with our front line troops. There had only been a few shells over, when "Stretcher Bearers" was shouted, and out I had to go, and along the front line for about 100 yards, where I found one of our chaps badly wounded. In trying to dodge one trench mortar, he had run right into another one, and he was literally peppered all over with small pieces of shrapnel, some had even passed through both his cheeks. Frankly, I didn't know where to start bandaging him up, and from his appearance, he seemed to be almost past human aid, so I made him as comfortable as I could, and bathed his face wounds. It may be unpleasant to write of watching death steal over a person, but I do so here because this was the first time in my life that I had witnessed such a thing, and it remains embedded in my memory.

In a very short time, he commenced to twist and twirl himself about in the bottom of the trench, I tried to hold him still but failed, and from inarticulate sounds, his voice turned to groans, which sounded horrible coming through a mouth full of blood. This rather upset some of his pals, who had stood by to help if necessary, and they all went further down the trench out of hearing distance, leaving me alone with him. I should have probably have gone with them had it not been my job to stay. I was indeed relieved, when the poor fellow's end came, and we put him on the side of the trench, covered with a ground sheet, for we had to wait until dusk before we could take him down the line for burial, as we could not carry a stretcher along the front line without being seen by Fritz. All this time, the shells had been coming over near us, fortunately none near enough to harm myself. Phillips returned when things had quietened down, saying that it was impossible for him to return before, as the Germans were shelling the communication trench.

On December 18th, our (A) Coy was relieved in the front line, and we went back to reserve in dugouts near Le Gard Chateau this meant about a four mile walk across muddy fields. These dugouts were situated in a wide trench, which ran by the side of a road, and although a good way from the front line, we were not allowed to be on the road in daylight, as it was under German observation. This position was in the midst of several of our heavy batteries of guns, the booming of which disturbed us at times, but our greatest enemies were German shells searching for these batteries. The Chateau was in a ruined position, only a part of a tower standing, and quite close by, was Swan Chateau, in a similar state. The Coy men here rested by day, and did working parties to the front line at night, repairing the 'bashed in' trenches, I, going with one of these parties on the night of the 20th. The weather was very cold, and at times we had snow. Our rest was very short, as on December 21st we moved forward again, and relived D Coy in the front line, in pouring rain. Things were very lively up here, and we were shelled heavily, [the enemy] sending over a rain of shells for two minutes duration, at intervals of about fifteen minutes. Our gunners were also busy, and at 9.15 p.m. one of our own shells fell short, and smashed into a dugout in our front line, completely burying the occupants, a machine gun team. They were quickly dug out, but were all casualties, two being dead and four wounded. We had noticed some of the shells dropping short before, fortunately without harming anyone, and we put it down to defective fuses in the shells. We S.B's were busy nearly all night getting these casualties down to the Aid Post, but made up for it by sleeping until noon.

We had the usual afternoon trench mortar shelling, and one landing close by our dugout, made it rather unsafe, so in the evening we S.Bs went down the 'Wynde' communication trench found a place in the tunnels, and had a comfortable night. Working by the previous methods of reliefs, we gauged that we should not be in the front line for Christmas, and this proved correct, for on December 23rd, we were relieved by the 6th London Regt, but only moved a short distance back into Woodcote Farm ... Inside, the walls were built up with concrete, although a direct hit on top would have proved fatal for us inside. The floor was of bricks, a nice warm soft bed, and most of the night we spent stamping our feet to keep warm. The next morning, about 20 men were detailed for a day light working party repairing 'Thames St' communication trench, and I accompanied them. It was thought that our small party, would not attract Fritz's attention, (he could see over our lines for miles about here), and we went forward in pairs at 25 yards intervals.

We had just left the road, and were walking in a light railway track, which ran up to the line, when over came a salvo of shells, all of which dropped right in the track, breaking and twisting up the rails, as if they were pieces of tin. There was no doubt that these shells were intended for us, but fortunately they dropped in one of the intervals, and before the next lot dropped, we were yards away from this, rested under the canal bank to get our wind, and were glad when we eventually reached the trench, where we were out of Jerries' view. We managed to return unmolested by shells, and later in the day moved further back across country to the Le Gard Chateau position again. We found the whole battalion in dugouts in this area, Btn H.Q's being in the cellars at Swan Chateau. Our (S.B's) dugout, this time was quite close to the ruined tower, and was built up off the ground with sandbags – being roomy, just suited our needs for the next day.

Our first thoughts on waking the next morning, were 'Why this is Xmas Day, what can we do to celebrate it'? The previous evening's post had brought me a fine parcel, containing many luxuries, and for this Xmas Day I was determined to leave the army 'grub' alone, and live well. All troops were left to enjoy themselves as best they could, but the issued rations turned out to be even poorer than usual, and the dinner consisting of bully beef and hot water was an utter failure. How thankful I was to have my parcel, and the following is the menu to which we S.B's sat down. Breakfast 10 a.m, milk bread, butter, bacon, potted meat, mince pies, buns. Dinner 3.30 p.m, meatcake, Xmas Pudding (but no threepenny pieces, as usual). Tea 7 p.m, salmon, milk bread, mince pies and pastries. You will notice that these meal times were later than usual, this is because in between meals we were munching nuts and fruit, and when the correct meal hour arrived, we did not feel hungry. This Xmas morning was damp and very windy, and things were exceedingly quiet – not a shot or shell could be heard, and it appeared that both sides must be thinking of 'Peace on earth, goodwill to amongst'. However, punctually at 1 p.m. a battery close to us commenced firing, and out of curiosity I kept count – exactly 40 shells were fired. Fritz kept quiet until the evening, when he repaid us with thanks, doing much damage to a railway track and dump close by us.

We celebrated the evening in a proper sort of way, by going to the Aid Post (in a small room at Swan Chateau), and having a sing-song. It was 11.15 before we returned to our dugout, and even then we had not finished, and we were all bright and lively until 1.15. We had a special treat on Boxing Day – a bath – this we had in the cellars of Swan Chateau, and was the first since December 1st – I'm sure we needed it. On December 27th Toby and I accompanied a working party, whose duty it was to convoy rations and fuel to the troops in the front line from Lankhoff Dump on the main road. Small trucks which ran on a light railway track were used, each truck being well loaded up and pushed up the line by 4 men. The whole of this track was under German machine gun fire, and when these opened out, our boys sheltered behind the trucks – it was a common thing, when in the line to open a sandbag of rations and find a bullet stuck in a loaf of bread. This job extended from 10 p.m. to 2.30 a.m. but we were used to these midnight 'dos' and it was only the cold that we minded. The next day 28th, Fritz was busy again shelling near our dugout with heavies – unfortunately one of our chaps, Ward by name, was hit in the chest by a piece of shrapnel, only a small wound, but it proved fatal, as he died shortly afterwards while we were dressing him in a dugout. We had orders to see that our gas masks were in good condition, as our Intelligence Corps had reported the presence of gas cylinders in the German front line; however nothing came of this scare.

After almost a month of living in dugouts and tunnels, we were at last relieved on December 29th by the 18th London Irish Rifles, and returned to Dominion Camp. We found the mud worse than ever, but it was a relief to be able to get about again after our confinement in trenches.

Like so many of the soldiers in this book, Dunham was especially interested in meeting people from his home 'community', in his case acquaintances from Norfolk:

Gardiner, a Diss lad, was killed near Ypres on February 10th 1917, and I assisted to bury him … On one of these working parties, I came across 2nd Lt Percy Peebles, an old City of Norwich School pal, who was in charge of a similar party from another battalion. We had quite a long 'pow-wow' together, and by appointment met on several evenings subsequently. After leaving Havre, he did fine work with his battalion, but was unfortunately killed whilst leading a raid at Arras in April 1917 …

It was curious, that on the very day when I was 'groggy', lying in blankets, a Norwich friend of mine, should discover my whereabouts and visit me. I refer to the visit of Reggie Cook, who was a signaller, on the Brigade Staff of the 4th Division. We had both known that our respective divisions were holding the line at the same time, however, this had happened, and he had managed to find me. Of course I couldn't go for a stroll with him, so he had to sit beside me, and we had a good old 'chin-wag' together.

By doing this, Dunham was able to introduce a sense of familiarity within his otherwise alien wartime experiences.

7

THE EARSHAM 'COMMUNITY'

Rural Norfolk was a very paternalistic society at the time of the First World War. The local squire often took an interest in men serving in the war, either his employees, or all the men in the village, and would often arrange for presents to be sent to the front. Meanwhile, the squire's own sons might well be at the front themselves as officers, but of course this did not mean they were any safer; the casualty rate among junior officers was even higher than that for men in the ranks.

The most well-known group of estate workers to join up as a group is that of the Sandringham estate. Frank Beck, born in 1861, was land agent on the royal estate there. He led the men of the estate ('E' Company, 5th Battalion, Norfolk Regiment, Territorial Force) into battle at Gallipoli on 12 August 1916. The men disappeared and their fate for a while unknown; after the Armistice, their bodies were found 800 yards behind the Turkish front line.

Earsham is a good example of a village dominated by its hall. The local squire, John Percy Meade, sent out gifts of tobacco to men of the village serving in the war, while his wife Helena knitted 'comforts' for them. The two sons of the house, John Wyndham Meade (born 1894) and Robert Percy Meade (born 1898) both served as officers, and Robert paid the ultimate price: he was killed in action on 11 July 1916, aged just twenty. He has no known grave but is commemorated on the Thiepval memorial. The Meades had one daughter, Helena Theodosia Kathleen Meade ('Dosia'), who was sixteen when war broke out. Unlike many girls of her class, she does not appear to have engaged in nursing work, but to have helped her mother at home. This may have been because she was not well herself – she died in 1919, also aged only twenty.

Unusually, the 'thank you' letters of the men on the estate to the squire and his family survive; they give a vivid picture of this relationship, and also of the experiences of these countrymen going to war for the first time. Unlike the Sandringham men, they served in many different regiments, though the Norfolk Regiment naturally predominated. The most prolific writer was J. Edward Hayes, gardener at Earsham Hall. At thirty-two, he was older than many of the raw recruits, but he joined up as soon as war was declared. His letters describe what happened:

9th Battalion, Norfolk Regiment, The Camp, Shoreham, 2 October 1914:
I have had a bad cold but am pleased to say it is much better now. Also that I have been enouculated [sic] today, also Fred has too. It was done in the arm but I find it very painfull at present. It is a very good idea for us to prevent the fever so much. We are getting on with the drills, we are got as far as rifle drill. I don't mind it so much now as I did at first, it's getting a bit easier for us now. It is splendid weather here, we could not wish for a better time in camping. They are trying to make us comfortable as far as they can. I thought that I saw Mr Wyndham here the other day at first sight but found it was not him. There are several young officers here.

Alma Barracks, Blackdown, Surrey, 24 August 1915:
I returned back to Camp quite safe but that we are under orders to leave here next Monday, which I expect will mean we are for France. The news in the papers has looked a great deal better this last four days, it would be great thing to think it was all finished but still we all must try our best. If there be any chance at all I will write to you, if only a line. When I was at Earsham the gardens looked well except for the weeds which cannot be helped in such bad times. F Pointer is quite well, he has not had his leave as the rest are only getting 48 hours.

Brighton, 22 December 1914:
I trust you will excuse me for not coming to see you when I was over last week. It was such a wet day on Sunday and I returned to Norwich on Monday. I saw Bayfield in Norwich on the Saturday and he told me you were out shooting early on Monday, and as I had several relations and friends to see, the time soon passed away. When I returned to Shoreham I was sent to Brighton with the two officers that I have to attend to. I am also pleased to say that I have a comfortable home which is a good thing for us. Fred Pointer is still left at Shoreham. We are getting on fairly well with the drills but have not been through a course of firing yet.

Brighton, 29 December 1914:
It is with great pleasure that I wish to return many thanks for the pipe and tobacco, also will you thank Mrs Meade for the muffler, also Miss Dosia for the mittens, as I was very pleased with them all … There are a good many of us have colds here, we don't seem to get much settled weather here, it is nearly always raining and we get it rough from off the sea. We cannot get on very fast with our drills owing to the weather. There are a lot of us billeted out here, all different regiments. Lawyer Cadge at Loddon has a son here as an officer. There is also a Lady living in Brighton which has some relatives at Caistor Rectory: having found that I know that part she is very good to us.

Alma Barracks, Blackdown, Surrey, 15 July 1915:
We are getting a lot of wet here as it seems a lonely place, proper military, nothing but barracks, as I make no doubt you know what it is. We are seven miles from Aldershot. We have been down here just a month and my battalion has started their course of firing this week which

I expect my company will take their turn next week. I have been down to look at the ranges today and find that we are not far from Bisley Ranges. I trust that I shall be able to make a good shot for I have done fairly well in the miniature ranges at Shoreham, got a two inch group which was not so bad. As stated by the officers we have lost a good many of our young officers from this battalion and are transferred to the centre at Colchester. I am afraid by what I can hear that we shall not be so very long before we get the order for the front as I think by what I can see that the men have set their minds to do their best. It's most astonishing to notice how the young fellow have pulled themselves together which I think is a good idea to have a certain amount of training in the years after this war is over in case of another break out it will not come so hard to the men. I myself don't mind it now as I did at first which I found was very hard. But still at the same time gardening is the best. I saw some very fine gardens down at Reigate time we were billeted there. I had the pleasure of looking round one large place which made think of Earsham and home. How has the rock garden looked this season and all the rest of the crops. I am not sure if we are getting another leave after we have been through our firing. If so I will try my best to pay you a visit as I should like to have another glance at the place before ewe go to the front.

A few weeks later, Hayes was writing from France:

BEF, Monday, no date:
I have got a cold but I am pleased to say I am still alive as we have had some very rough times. Plenty of wet as the trenches are in a terrible state. We are expecting to be in them again this week. I have been looking for a letter from you for some time as I should like to hear how things are going on at Earsham as I am afraid there will want several more of them out here by another spring.

BEF, France 3 October 1915:
I wish to return many thanks for the parcel which you and Mrs Meade sent to me. I received it quite safe. I hope these few lines will meet you and all in the best of health as I am fit and well after coming out of the trenches. There were plenty of shells and bullets flying about. We are being relieved for a time. We lost some of our men. Mr Finch that lives at Catton was wounded. As I make no doubt you have heard the news by now. It would be a great idea if it could all be settled before the winter set in as this is not too good a country for rough weather. F Pointer was alright the last time I saw him. I have no particular news to tell you as I should like to hope you will excuse me for writing with pencil and untidy letter as very inconvenient to get our wants at the present time.

BEF, 25 February 1916:
Having just a few minutes to spare I now have the pleasure of writing a few lines to you, trusting they will meet you in the best of health, as it leaves me, fairly well but have had a cold also a touch of my rheumatism, which has been very uncomfortable for me as we do not get quite so much comfort out here as we should in private life but am pleased to say it is far better just at present. We have had a very warm time here just lately with shells and shrapnel but the trenches are in a little better order than they used to be. I trust you will excuse me for not writing before …

Many thanks for the Xmas gift and the cigarettes which I got quite safely. I see by the papers there has been an air [raid] on Lowestoft last Sunday. We don't seem safe wherever we are. I expect you have not got many in the gardens now as everything must be very backward. It would be a grand thing for us all to know when all the world is at peace again. For I myself shall never forget the terrible sights I have witnessed what with the war and the ruins, but thank God he has spared me up to the present and I trust he will for me to see the end. I expect that Mr Wyndham has gone to a very dangerous part of the line according to your last letter, and Master Robert ... I have not seen F Pointer for some time. I was quite surprised to hear you had sold your horses and got motors in their place.

BEF, 10 May 1916:
Just a few lines in answer to your last letter which I was very pleased to receive, but was sorry to hear that you have not been well and confined to your room as it was a very rough time with the weather and winds when you wrote to me but I trust the weather is more suitable for you at present. We have had some fine and hot days out here but suddenly another change. We have finished our rest and have got back to the trenches again, which they seems to be got more dangerous from the German artillery and machine guns than when we went away, but I am very thankful to say I am fairly fit and still quite safe. We are all looking for that peaceful day to come but am afraid that will not be yet as England means to master them for their brutality and destroy their army to keep them quiet in years to come.

Would you mind doing me a favour by thanking Mrs Meade for her parcel and letter which I was very pleased to receive, trusting she is in good health and spirits for it's a heavy strain on one's mind to know they have sons doing their duty for King and Country. I also hope to hear that Mr Wyndham and Master Robert are both quite safe and Miss Dosia is in perfect good health. It seems ages to me since I was in England. Please remember me to all that enquires after me. I hope to have a leave in a short time of which I hope to pay a visit but am afraid shall hardly know some of the places done by the hurricane, sorry to hear you have the best of your trees fallen that is mostly the case. The rock garden I expect is looking very gay. There seems to be a good show of fruit about here when we come across trees, but the houses are completely ruins for Belgium has suffered heavily.

BEF, 9 August 1916:
As I have not heard from you since I wrote last it is with the greatest of pleasure that I have few minutes to spare to write a line or two trusting that they will meet you and all in good health, as it leaves me still quite safe
[Here four lines have been crossed through, presumably by the censor]
As regards to the weather it's been very trying with the heat but am very pleased to say that we seem to be getting the best of them now which I trust they will soon be beaten for I am sure everybody is looking for that happy day of peace to come, but we must thank our munitions workers to put off their holidays and keep us going with plenty of shells, which for my part is a great benefit to the infantry man by not having so many casualties as the first part of the war. One really cannot realise only them that are amongst it what a terrible sight it look around us. I hear of some very sad news which I hope is not true that has fallen upon you of Master Robert being wounded and then missing, and the last report he is dead.

Also that Mr Wyndham has been wounded, again hoping that he is getting the better of his wounds, and all do pull through.

PS: F Pointer was quite well the last time I saw him.

BEF, 14 September 1916:

I wish to return my deepest sympathy in your sad bereavement of losing Mr Robert and to all the family in this terrible war. I expect that Mrs Meade feels it very much and very glad to hear Mr Wyndham has got better of his wounds. As for myself I must say that I am still quite safe and feel fairly well although we are in a very warm position just at present which I trust God will keep me safe through it all to the end and give me health and strength to do my duty. We came past the place where Mr Robert was buried. Fred Pointer was still alright the last time I saw him. I was not at all surprised to hear that you would have to make some arrangements in the gardens for there are not the hands to carry it all on …

I saw in the papers where the Zepps had visited Norfolk again. I hope and trust that it will soon be brought to an end for us seems to be gaining victory at every point. I hope that I shall not have another winter out here.

The Fred Pointer referred to several times by Hayes was another employee who joined up in the first wave. He wrote from 9th Norfolk Battalion's training camp at Shoreham.

We are having rather a rough time down here now for we are still under canvas and it is forever raining. We have not had a lot of cold weather yet as this is rather a warm climate. It was lovely down here when we first came down.

We are getting on pretty well with our training but have not done any firing yet for we have only got some old rifles to train with. We are doing bayonet fighting now and route marches and entrenching, shall be glad when we do some firing as that is the chief thing. I expect Master Wyndham is in training by now, most of our officers are very young but they are very nice.

Hayes is quite well and getting on alright. I don't know when we are going into our own huts they are building for us as they are such a long while finishing them. It takes a long time to build them for 23,000 troops. There are several chaps down here that I know from my home so I have plenty of company. I don't think, sir, this war can last much longer, they may hold through the winter and then in the spring we can soon finish them off as we shall have plenty of trained men by then.

A few months later he was in Brighton, having tried to visit the Hall on his recent leave.

Thank you so much for the present you sent me also Mrs Meade and Miss Dosia, You will think it very unkind of me for not writing before but I only got it this week as all our letters and parcles [sic] had been stopped here as nearly all our chaps were here, and we only came this week and some of them are gone to take our places. We had a very nice time at Shoreham at Xmas there was only 100 of us down there. I have got a splendid billet here all by myself.

Was so sorry I did not see you when I came over as you were out shooting and Mrs Meade was out too. We have not done very little training lately as the weather has been so bad, so we shall have to make up for it now, The King and Queen were down here yesterday and we had to line the streets, it was a fine sight. I don't think I have any more news this time.

Three letters and one postcard survive from Pointer in France, all in return for gifts sent by the Meades:

[Undated]:
Many thanks to you and Mrs Meade for Parcle received quite safe. I got it just as I was leaving England and it came quite useful. Was sorry could not write before, I told Hayes to tell you I got it quite safe as I left 2 days before him. Sorry was unable to come and see you when I was at home but I only had 48 hours leave as it was a quick move. The weather was dreadful here last week, it rained nearly every day. Hayes told me he came over and saw you when he was at home, I should have liked to come too.

Expect Mr Windham is back out here now? Was glad he was not wounded serious.

[Undated]:
Many thanks for your gift of cigarettes and tobacco which I received quite safely. Such gift shows your appreciation for us soldiers who are fighting for our Country's Honour.

[Undated]:
Many thanks for Parcle received quite safe, was very pleased with it. Private Hayes is quite well, he shew me the letter he had from Captain Meade, was sorry to hear he had been ill, hope he is quite well again now. We have had a very rough winter out here but the weather is better now, but very changeable. Shall be glad when the war is over so we can get back to England again.

France, 13 January 1916, addressed to Mrs Meade:
Many thanks for cigarettes received quite safe, they are a great comfort out here. We are having rather rough weather, so much wet and such a lot of mud. Hope you and Captain Meade are quite well, as it leaves me. Hope this job will soon be over so I can get back again.

Another local family was named Jolly, and they received much kindness from the Meades, as the letters show:

Private H. Jolly, 12 December 1914:
In answer to yours of the 7th I take the opportunity of answering your kind and welcome letter. I must first of all thank you for interesting yourself in the welfare of my Wife and Children, and I must thank you for letting her have the Cottage free of rent. And now I wish to tell you that during the last fortnight or so I have received letters from my Wife which have been delayed in some way or other and have been dated back as far as October, so you will now understand why I wrote home telling her that I had not received any letters of late. I am also very pleased to hear that Dr and Mrs Bindley has been to see her. I have not received the Pipe and Tobacco yet but I shall no doubt get it in due course. I might say that I am in the best of health and I hope that you are the same. So I will close this letter thanking you once again for your kindness and wishing you all a Merry Christmas and a Happy New Year.

Private H. Jolly, Cavalry Base Camp, Rouen, France, undated:
Arrived back quite safely, we had rather a rough voyage over, but we had rather a jolly time on board. Since I have been off furlough, I went in hospital, with an internal complaint, but nothing very serious.

I am quite better now, am waiting orders to rejoin my regiment again. Down here we only have an issue of tobacco once a week, we get four ounces of tobacco, but I don't smoke a pipe, so I am rather handycapt [sic] without cigarettes'.

The weather here is grand so far, we get an occasional shower, but nothing to speak of. We have got plenty of work to do, because we have our horses down here.

Private H. Jolly, BEF, France, 19 September 1915:
I received your postcard quite alright. I was very sorry to hear you had sent me a parcel and it had been returned. The reason I did not get it was I had been in hospital and was at the base. But if you intend to send the parcel the above address will find [me] alright. I must thank you for the kind way you treat my wife and help to cheer up as it is a great comfort to her. We are having quite satisfactory weather out here at present.

Jolly survived the war, but a William Jolly, a gunner in the Royal Garrison Artillery, died on 6 July 1918. He was forty-six years of age and might have been the brother, or even the father, of Private Jolly.

Another Earsham man, John High, was not so fortunate:

Private John High, Cinder City, Le Havre, 20 September 1915:
I thank you very much for parcel which I received quite safe. Yes it is very sickening having to be down here so long but I shall have to be content here for some time yet, I wish we could hear this cruel war all over. I am glad to hear Mr Wyndham's wound is very well I hope it will soon be quite alright.

I was surprised to hear Mr Robert is out in France. I think both Mr Wyndham and Mr Robert have shown a good example to the young men of Earsham. I hope and trust they will both be spared to come back quite safe.

We are having very nice weather now I hope it is the same at home so they can get harvest in alright.

Private High was killed in action on 28 April 1917 and is commemorated on the Arras Memorial.

The Threadgold family had several members in the forces, including Sidney, wounded early in the war.

Sidney Threadgold, Military Hospital, Chatham, 2 March 1915:
I felt it my place to write to you thanking you for the hat-cover which is very useful. We have had plenty of rain down here and it has come in very handy. I must also thank you very much for the scarf which came very handy when I was warned for guard especially of a night time. My pipe comes in very handy for an enjoyable smoke when off duty. You will see by the above address I am in hospital with my wound again. It has been discharging again but I hope it will soon be well again. The cause of it is there is a piece of broken bone in my forehead. As soon

as I am well I expect I shall be off to France again which I don't mind when it is my turn again. I say you have only to die once and you might as well die on the battlefield as in a feather bed.

Sidney Threadgold, Military Hospital, Whitworth Street, Manchester, 29 December 1915:
I now take the greatest of pleasure in writing to you with my left hand thanking you for the cigarettes, which you kindly sent to me. I am glad to say I am progressing favourably.

Sidney Threadgold, Machine Gun section, Middlesex Regiment, undated:
I hope you will not think I am taking a liberty in writing these few lines to you, but I thought it my place to do so as you were so good to me when I was home wounded. I am now in about one of the hottest parts of the firing line. I daresay you can guess the place. Of course I would like to tell you where it is but we are not allowed to. I have gone back on my old job and I must tell you I have had some awful experiences but ...

I am sent out here to do my duty and I must do it with a good heart. I am fighting with my comrades for a just cause and we must stick it until the very end. My brother Frank is home but I am glad to say he is not wounded but has appendicitis and I trust as soon as he is better and strong he will come back here again. This country where I am is in a shocking condition, the place is all in ruins. We have smashed the cathedral also the cloth hall. The cloth-hall is a kind of a stock-exchange. I only hope that we have the pleasure of getting into Germany but I am afraid it will be a long time before we do.

Sidney died on 2 September 1918 and was buried in Earsham churchyard. One of his brothers, Albert, had already died, killed in action on 19 October 1916, and he is remembered on the Arras Memorial. The Earsham war memorial has the names of twenty-five men killed in the war, including Percy Robert Meade, John High, Albert and Sidney Threadgold, and no doubt others who worked on the Earsham Hall estate. The letters give us a real sense of these ordinary Norfolk estate workers, each one equally worthy of honour and respect.

8

THE CARROW 'COMMUNITY'

Other 'communities' were based around a place of work. The largest employer in Norfolk was probably Colman's, the food manufacturing firm, best known for its mustard. Its house magazine carried several pages of letters from soldiers serving abroad, who were especially pleased when they met another ex-Colman worker or when they saw one of the firm's products in some far-flung corner of the world. Their letters give vivid descriptions of their new lives:

In Training or in Hospital in England

Rifleman W. S. Jones, Oswestry, 21 November 1916:
I often think of the pleasant days I spent at [the Colman's London works in] Cannon Street, and wonder how things are going on these days. Doubtless there have been a number of changes in the staff since I took my departure. It was with deep regret that I heard from Mr Scotcher, of the death of Mr Aldrich's son at the front, and should be glad if you will convey to Mr Aldrich my deepest sympathy in his sad bereavement. It is very sad to think of all these valuable lives being sacrificed, and we can but trust that they are not being sacrificed in vain.

As for myself, I am glad to say that I am keeping very well, in spite of the hard training and bad weather. We have had a very stiff training, and after three months I was termed a fully-trained man. My brother, who has been in this Regiment for a considerable time, is now in the same hut as me. We managed to get into the same Musketry class, and after about three weeks on musketry, we went to Bettisfield in Flint to 'fire our course' ... I also applied for, or rather on behalf of, my brother, with the result that the day we returned from leave, we were both put into the 'Flag Wavers' or Signal Section. I am simply delighted with the work, and although it will entail a lot of study, it is a very pleasant change after so much squad drill and rifle exercises.

I understand that the signalling course takes about four months. We have to learn how to send and read messages in the Morse code, on the telephone, flag, lamp, and disc. We also study the construction of the telephone, how to lay the lines, map reading, despatch riding, and numerous subjects ...

Private A. H. Cornwell, RAMC, near Doncaster, 28 November 1916:
I must thank you very much for the Magazine you have sent me. It is always a pleasure to read them, for it makes one think of the good old days down at the Works. I have passed them on to some of our chaps, and they think they are just grand ... I was glad to read that Captain G. R. Colman is progressing in health, and hope he will soon be restored to health and strength again. I was not sorry when we left camp, for it was terrible up there the last three weeks. It rained in torrents nearly every day, but we are at a nice place now ...

Sapper E. H. Gillings, Weybourne, 22 December 1916:
It is very nice indeed to have the Magazine as usual, and very interesting to read the letters that have been sent to you and other friends at Carrow from the men now serving in the Army, many of whom I know quite well ... I have only one Norwich man with me here, and he did not work at Carrow, but however many of my friends are quite eager to read it, and I shall lend it to them in turns ... This place is only a small country village, with nowhere in particular to go after the day's duty, and I can assure you it is in such a place as this that one learns of the real value of the YMCA huts ...

Driver A. Cruickshanks, St John's Hospital, Southport, 28 December 1916:
I am writing to thank you for the Magazine, and I must say I was very pleased to receive it and the photograph of the entrance to the works. It reminds me of the old days when I used to be on duty there. I am sorry to see that so many men have fallen in this great war which were connected with the Firm ... I hope to be out of hospital soon and come and give you all a look ...

Bombardier Bert H. Wright, High Wycombe, 6 February 1917:
There is one of the Carrow boys stationed here who has returned from Egypt, and he always greets me with the remark, 'Well, don't forget, Bomb, to pass the Magazine on when you get it.' The boys of the Mustard Mill will remember him. His name is Bloomfield, and he was also in the Band. After I had been stationed in High Wycombe for five months, I was picked out and sent to Aldershot, there to go through a course of 'Physical training and Bayonet Fighting', for which I won a (V. G.) Certificate, therefore qualifying me an instructor for that work, which, after being again set to Wycombe, I have been doing since ...

Private H. Turner, RAMC, Blackpool, 1917:
We are sleeping under canvas, and the first night we were flooded out, the water being six inches deep, so we were up all night. We only arrived here on Friday night, but by 12 am on Saturday we had been inoculated, vaccinated and served out ... khaki, boots etc. We are finished now, with the exception of a belt and stick. Next week we begin serious operations, we are told – lectures and drilling from 6.30 to 4, so you see we shall be busy ...

In France

Private J. R. Dawson of the Queen's Westminsters to C. R. Aldrich, published in *Carrow Works Magazine,* April 1915:
My Christmas was the most eventful I have ever or am ever likely to spend. What I shall now write will doubtless seem incomprehensible but it is nevertheless perfectly true. On Christmas Eve a regular battalion on our left exchanged Christmas greetings with the enemy who were entrenched about 200 yards away. Several men went out and met them half-way, exchanging cakes for wines etc. Two men from this battalion and two from my own company managed to get unarmed into the German trenches, but as they had evidently seen too much they were kept as 'souvenirs'. No shots were fired during the night. On Christmas Day practically the whole of our battalion spent the morning and afternoon in conversing and exchanging souvenirs with those of the enemy on our front. These were three Saxon Regiments and were decent fellows. Personally I succeeded in obtaining a 1 pfenning piece, a tunic button, an autograph postcard and a mouth organ, in exchange for one of our buttons, a signed card and some chocolate. Several of their officers also conversed with our own, while two or three photographs were taken.

Private A. J. Knights, BEF, France, 4 December 1915:
I am writing to you to give you an idea of what it is like going to the trenches from our rest billets and life in the trenches … We generally leave our rest billets during the morning, as we have about eight miles to march. You would hardly think we were soldiers, for as you can guess we have not that clean appearance which a soldier has in England, as the roads are in such a bad condition with the heavy transports always on them. We tie sandbags over our putties to keep them as clean as possible, and we get an old sock or glove to put over the breech of our rifles. We march away in sections of fours, until we get within about a mile of the communication trench, then we plod along in single file over a very bad path full of shell holes. When we get in sight of the flares of our own and the enemies, we have to be very careful: perhaps when we get to the communication trench we get under a rather hot shell fire and we have to lie down in the mud for a time; after this is over we wind our way down the trenches, our packs catching each side of the trench, so as to make it very difficult to walk. At last we reach the trench that we are to spend the next few days in; it may be in reserve, or supports, or right in the firing line. The firing line is subject to whizz-bangs; these are shells we dread the most. We can't hear them coming along like the ordinary ones; they come just over the parapet, and cut our dug-outs to pieces if they get a lucky hit.

Private Bertram C Mead, BEF, France, 9 January 1916:
The rain for the past two months has been wet: rain, rain, rain, with monotonous regularity. Even gloomy old Manchester is not in it compared with Sunny (?) France in the winter months. We have had some rather trying spells in the trenches, at times waist-deep in mud and water, but endless labour has now improved them somewhat, and we can wade about in wading boots with some degree of comfort. At times it has been no uncommon occurrence for men to become so firmly embedded that the assistance of a digging party has been necessary before extrication was possible.

Private Leslie Crump, BEF France, 18 November 1916 [to his father]:
I expect by now you will have received my field card stating that I have been admitted to hospital wounded. I got a piece of shrapnel in the back of my head, but it was not very serious, and am now at a convalescent home having quite a good time. I went over the top with the regiment on Monday and again on Tuesday morning. We have been in the latest heavy fighting, and as no doubt you have seen by the papers were very successful in gaining our objective. I am sorry to say that our regiment suffered rather severely, and consider myself exceedingly fortunate in escaping as I did ... I was in the fighting region for seventy-two hours, during that time I existed on a tin of bully beef, a few biscuits and a bottle of water; the whole time I didn't get a wink of sleep, so you can be sure I was not sorry to get to hospital and get some sleep and something to eat. I saw Young a few hours before I was hit, and he was quite all right. I could almost write a book on the happenings of the last few days, but I think I have told you everything I am able to.

I am in a fine place now, good food and accommodation, away from the sound of the guns, and am having quite a good rest before joining up the regiment again ...

Sapper R. W. Cant, BEF, France, December 1916:
Since the last time I wrote I have been shifted about a good bit... I was sent down to base and stopped there for about two months. From there I was sent to the 2nd Cavalry Brigade ... I am now with the 2nd Anzac Corps. These men of course were out in the Dardanelles ...

Our officers are very good to us. The other day they bought us a 'Decca' gramophone with about forty records. At night times we all get round the fire and listen to it. It often brings back to us the memories of home ...

Private A. Farrow, 29 December 1916:
I have the pleasure of saying that we are having six weeks rest from the trenches. And it is a pleasure you may guess now that the cold weather has now set in. I might tell you that I spent at least two good hours reading the Magazine on Boxing night after I had done work, and I had five more of my mates looking over my shoulders, enjoying the pictures and news, and they all give the Editor the highest praise for his good work, and I think that all the boys in my platoon have read and enjoyed it ... My light is getting very low, which is a candle between six writers so I must conclude my short letter ...

Section Lieutenant W. E. Daniel, BEF, France, 26 January 1917:
We arrived in Havre about three in the morning, and proceeded to Harfleur, where we are at present. We shall be leaving tomorrow, but letters will be forwarded to wherever we go.
Yesterday I went through about forty yards of gas, which was exceedingly powerful, but I did not feel any ill effects to speak of ...

I shall be very glad to have the Carrow Magazine sent out to me and any literature you can spare, as I fully expect to be in a dug-out soon, and away from any town ...

Sapper W. Rix, BEF, France 1917:
We often see different adverts when on the march, such as 'Colman's Mustard is the best', only it is in French, and as I am not a linguist I cannot pronounce it ...

I used to grumble about the old Fibre House jobs, but some of these jobs out here are a trifle worse, but we just keep on smiling, you know, and look out for the better times to come. I met young Tom Hardy a few months back at the Somme, and we had a real good time together. He was quite well, and wished to be remembered to you all if I wrote at any time …

Private R. L. Winter, BEF France, 22 July 1917:
We have been out here just over a month now. The first fortnight we were at the Base at Havre, now we are about twenty miles behind the line, and having a good time … There is not much work to do, only guards and fire picquets. We have a tennis and cricket club, and there is plenty of swimming and fishing to be had … The Fire Engine is kept in a very large garden, with plenty of fruit, which we have stewed for dinner or supper. We have eggs and bacon for breakfast. My French is coming in very useful. I shall soon speak like a native…

Alfred Heald, Friends' Ambulance Unit, France, 3 August 1917: Written by candle light at 2 pm on floor of billets in loft, in which 16 sleep, a small sort of combined stable and house, about the size of the motor and fowl house at home.

Private R. L. Winter, BEF, France, 1 August 1917:
Up at 6 am, and in 'Mary' off to communication trench, raining hard, awful mud, plenty of shell holes in roads; saw French and German wounded brought up, then off to dressing station, a perfect little dug-out, telephones and electric light. 'Mary' protected by wall of sandbags while waiting, then off to Field Hospital, magnificent place, tents and wooden huts, splendidly efficient doing essential operations, then back to billet; firing going on all the time, have two gas masks and the blue French trench helmet. Wet through and covered with mud. Moved into a billet in a garret: roads all screened. 1 pm lunch and then to D and back to V E and back to billets; 230 kilometres altogether, about 150 miles, rain and mud all the time, no lights for some miles near billets, drive by shell-fire light, arrived back by 12.30 pm … For miles from here only soldiers to be seen, all other people chased away, except one old limping woman. Shelled all night, one landed in field at back of quarters, another smashed house a few doors away … The appearance of the line at night is worse by far than the most gruesome picture of Dante's 'Inferno'.
   Am fit and happy.

Bombardier E. G. Hill, 11 September 1917:
Not far away the growl of the guns reaches you, and you think hard. Aeroplanes go buzzing overhead, obviously very busy. Troops, motor lorries, waggons, mules, limbers, and guns. Each and every man wears a shrapnel hat, and has a gas helmet slung on his shoulder. Nobody is excited, everything is in order, military police control the traffic, we join the throng and are lost in the endless stream. But we come out all right and find our quarters and position in due course.
   One's first experience under shell fire is not too pleasant. I cannot quite describe the feeling, but it is hardly fear. Doubtless its effects taken in individual cases vary a good deal, but one soon becomes accustomed to the whistle and bursting of the various shells, and soon acquires a fairly accurate knowledge as to the distance a shell is likely to burst from you, and, having judged, if you decide it is near at hand, you take the best cover possible, and, what is more, you

move to it pretty sharp. Failing cover, down you go, flat as a plaice, mud, slush, and water are all the same, it's flat you want to get, you breathe hard, wait for the crash, and take your chance. It is advisable to remain prone for at least ten seconds after the burst, as pieces go a fair height, and while flat your shrapnel helmet protects your head and neck …

All Pals Together

A group of letters from the front received by Mr C. R. Aldrich show colleagues at work becoming comrades-in-arms:

A. G. Arkoll, 6 April 1915:
I thought you would be interested to hear that I was now in France. We have been out a little over a fortnight now, and Moylan and Goosey, and one or two others from the office, are in the same division. No doubt you have heard from them. I saw Moylan just before leaving Watford, and Goosey and two other men, whose names I forget, at the Baths the other day in a town near to us. They take us in Companies once a week to some coal mines where they have hot shower baths fitted up for the miners. I can assure you they are very much appreciated by the troops. We are moving up nearer to the firing line tomorrow, and no doubt shall have a turn in the trenches within a few days. We are at present in a small village, and seem quite cut off from everything English except the *Daily Mail* Continental edition, which we can obtain the day after publication for 1½ d a copy. My friends here have suggested that I should ask you to send us a tin of mustard occasionally, as we have not been able to obtain any since our arrival in France. They don't seem to sell it in this part of the country, and only a very small quantity of the French variety.

F. E. Moylan, Trenches, 18 April 1915:
Many thanks for the copy of the 'Carrow Works Magazine'. I got it just as we were going into the trenches on Easter Saturday afternoon, so of course I didn't get any time to read it then, but on Monday (when we had rain all day) I had an opportunity, and was extremely interested in the two letters from Dawson, especially with regard to the Christmas "truce". At present I am not right up at the firing line, but quite close enough to hear the guns, and see the star bombs at night. I have not, of course, been in the trenches when any big action has been in progress; in fact, in the daytime on one occasion I sat all day without firing a shot, smoking. resting and sleeping – quite war de luxe. Last Wednesday, I had the good luck to come across Goosey. As I was on the march I could only manage to shake hands and ask one or two hurried questions, but anyway I was jolly pleased to see him, and kept an eye out for Barnett and Williams, but did not see either of them. I think the most exciting thing I have seen out here was an aeroplane fight. One morning six machines were at it 'hammer and tongs' but unfortunately I did not see any German come to grief. Another time I counted forty-seven shots fired at a French machine, and a fellow near me counted as many as 165; it is very easy to count these shots, as each one gives off a ball of white smoke which keeps intact for a long time and floats away as a kind of little cloud on its own: if the sky is clear the appearance is very peculiar. After the rather rough weather at Easter we are now enjoying quite summerlike days, and you may be sure they are enjoyed as fully as they can be in the circumstances.

Herbert C. Maben, 18 April 1915:

It is six weeks ago today since I left London. We arrived behind the firing line on Saturday March 13th. Here we were put into billets which were really derelict farmhouses. My first sleep was certainly not an easy one, and I was quite glad to get up, even at 5.30 am. The line we have been holding does not consist of actual trenches, the ground being too swampy, but instead there is a sort of 'Grouse Butt' made with sandbags and connected by a barricade (also of sandbags) with the butts on either side. These have many advantages being dry, roomy and comfortable; but they also have some disadvantages, one being that they require considerable repairing, especially after the Germans have been sending over a few 'pip-squeaks' these latter being a kind of trench mortar fired from the opposite trench. The repairs are done by the Royal Engineers, but we have to do the fatigue work for them, and when that occurs we spend our time filling sandbags. The Germans opposed to us when we first arrived were Saxons, and one day they put a placard over the parapet with the words – 'We are Saxons, we won't fire if you won't fire.' They did not stay long however, and were relieved by a Prussian Regiment, who greeted us with 'John Bull, no good.' I expect the latter included a few waiters chucked out of England. Well, we spent a fortnight up at the firing line, then we came back for a week's rest, and then another fortnight up, and we are now resting again about eight or nine miles back from the front line.

So far I have been very fortunate, and have been as fit as a fiddle all the time. I have only had two really extraordinary experiences, one being when I was sleeping in a dug-out one day and without a word of warning it collapsed on top of me and another fellow. Help was soon forthcoming, and we were soon dug out of the dug-out not one bit the worse. The other occasion was when marching one night a shell whizzed over our heads and landed with a dull thud ten yards past us, but I am still alive to tell the tale.

Yesterday afternoon I got three hours' leave and went into a town about two miles away. The place was packed with military, all British. I went into a baker's shop to have some tea, and as I was sitting there with some of my friends in came some of the 20th London, amongst whom was none other than Goosey, looking in the pink of condition and smiling all over. He told me that Arkoll was somewhere in the town, so we immediately set out to find him. We found him billeted in a school *pour jeunes filles*. He was just going on guard, so we had only a moment or two with him. Still we were very glad to see each other. It was really extraordinary that the Export Invoice Department should meet *en bloc* somewhere in France, especially as we are all in different regiments. Williams and Barnett are also in the town, but I did not manage to see them.

It may interest you to know that we get jolly well fed out here, and when at rest we feed like fighting cocks. Just to give you an idea, today we had porridge, bacon, bread, butter, jam and tea for breakfast; for dinner we had curried stew, potatoes, boiled rice; and then we get tea about 5 o'clock, when we finish up the bread and jam we may or may not have over. Today being Sunday we had a service in an adjacent field conducted by a 'guid auld Scotch Meenister'.

I am writing this stretched full length in an orchard with the sun pouring down, and a gramophone, kindly lent by the officers, playing about ten yards to my rear. Well, you will think I am having a grand old time of it, and so I am, though there *are* times which we try to forget as quickly as possible. I have lost one pal already; the shot which accounted for him first of all pierced a sandbag then entered his back on the right side. He could not possibly have been seen as he was under cover at the time.

Fred Goosey, 2 May 1915:

Our Brigade has now taken up a portion of the line, and we have been going up into the trenches for forty-eight hours at a time, followed by forty-eight hours rest at a village three miles behind the line. Next time I believe we go up for four days, two in the firing line and two in support. That will probably be next Wednesday. That part of the line which we occupy is 200 yards from the Germans, and occasionally we partake of a little conversation with them, such as, 'Good morning, Fritz; had your breakfast?' They reply, 'Yes, who are you' etc. Sometimes they hoist up a placard on which is, 'We are Saxon, you are Anglo-Saxons, don't fire; wait till the Prussians come in.' It is rather quieter at this part of the line than where were before. We are not in ordinary trenches, but in breastworks, that is to say, barricades built up over the ground, as the ground is wet, or was wet, and couldn't be trenched. There is more room in these breastworks.

About a fortnight ago, when we stationed in a big town, two or three miles back, some of the Scottish came in. I ran across Maben, and as Arkoll's regiment was also there, Maben and I went round, and we held a little meeting of the Export department of J and J Colman.

Four of these men – Privates P. Barnett, F. Goosey, R. A. Williams and F. E. Moylan – were involved in fierce fighting in France on 25/26 September 1915. Barnett was killed but the others survived, although Goosey's elder brother was killed in the fighting.

Greece

Private A. R. Hill, somewhere in Macedonia, 8 January 1917:

I arrived at Salonika in November, and after a short stay we were moved further up country, where we are at present (somewhere in Macedonia), in a village surrounded by mountains. The weather out here at Christmas was fine and warm, more like summer than what we get at home. I am sorry to see so many of our comrades being added to the Roll of Honour. And express my sympathy to the relatives and friends of those who have fallen for the cause of Right and Liberty ...

Private S. H. Harris, Salonika, 10 February 1917:

As second Driver for a long time I'm having quite a good time out here, and see a lot of the country. Last week I was away from camp for five days, and often we are away for odd nights. During these trips the waggon is our home. You can imagine it is not quite up to the Ritz for sleeping in, when loaded with all sorts of things. I'm used to it now, and am afraid I shall have to buy one when I get home, so as to get a good night's sleep.

Palestine

Private G. Simmons, Palestine, 9 June 1917:

Eating is in the open-air system, eating, sleeping, and general living, and one is sorry, too, at times, especially during sand storms, which are the limit. Everything, including your food, is sand, which you cannot keep from anything. Eyes, ears and mouth are particularly the parts which are personally tormented; but it's all in the game I suppose, and it won't be a bad idea when they draw stumps and let us know the game is finished, what say you?

We get plenty of the other sport too, but I expect nothing to the western front, so I won't say much to that, although it puts the wind up at times; but it's really surprising what one *can* get used to. One wouldn't think it possible in pre-war days that one could get used to things which are parts of everyday life in these days of unrest and strife.

As regards snakes and scorpions, centipedes and vile spiders, etc, we get our turns with them; but snakes are not numerous, or if they are, one doesn't see many. I almost trod on one the day before the yesterday, as I was returning from inoculation, but it was off at a tremendous rate. They travel as fast as a man can run. It was a fine one, I should think easily 2 feet 6 inches in length, but I thought discretion the wisest thing, so let him off with a caution.

It's not quite as hot here as in Egypt, but plenty hot enough.

Bombardier Sydney W. Smith, Palestine, 16 August 1917:
Although for the past few months I have had to adopt the roving habits of the Bedouin, and have wandered about the Sinai Peninsula and Southern Palestine, yet I am glad to say the [Carrow] Magazine has eventually reached me; but upon perusing it, although glad to learn of these who have won honours, I am sorry for those who have fallen in battle, especially my old workmate, Walter Copland … Having spent a considerable time in the desert we are well climatised, but the heat at times is very trying, both to men and horses … Lucky is the man who has the fortune to bivouac for the night near one of the few oases there are in this district, for they have the opportunity of getting figs, grapes, pomegranates, prickly pears and dates, as these fruits are now in season …

India

Sergeant P. H. Brunskill, Lucknow, India, 20 November 1916:
We arrived off Dar-es-Salaam, until recently the principal seaport of German East Africa, but now occupied by British forces, on September 25th. We were then informed that the landing was to take place on the coast further south, and for this purpose sailed on the 27th. The next day I was taken ill and admitted into the ship's hospital and treated for heatstroke. The doctor would not allow me to go ashore, so when the troops were landed, the ship continued her voyage to Mombasa, the chief port of British East Africa, where on October 1st I was landed and taken to the base hospital … By October 14th I had sufficiently recovered to be included in a party of patients who were being transferred to the base hospital at Nairobi, the capital of British East Africa. Nairobi is 327 miles inland, and stands about 6,000 feet above sea level. It is therefore considered one of the most healthy districts in the colony, and a good many patients are transferred to finish their periods of convalescence …

The railway journey is an interesting one. It is possible to see all sorts of wild animals, including ostriches, zebras, giraffes, wild buck etc … We left Nairobi at 11 am on 30th October and arrived at Mombasa the following day, at once proceeding on board the steamer awaiting us. We left for Bombay about 4 pm. The nine days' sail across was very pleasant, the sea being remarkably calm ... I expect to be sent to join my unit when I get back to East Africa, as I am now quite fit again ...

Lucknow is a most interesting city. It has fine broad thoroughfares and is well named 'the Garden City'. The Residency, which figured so prominently during the famous siege, is a building standing in the midst of lovely grounds, and the marks made by the bullets coming into contact with the walls are still plainly to be seen.

In the Navy

Private J. Webster, RNAS, Howden, 2 January 1917: A sailor's life is rather different to selling DSF. Can you picture me as cook? Yes! That has been my occupation these last two days. I guess my wife would have laughed had she seen me cooking dinner today, which consisted of steak and onions, followed by bread pudding. I hadn't the least idea how to commence, but somehow I managed to get through, and there were no complaints. I get quite a miscellaneous collection of work to do ...

As these letters show, many of these men eagerly read the works' magazine to make them feel part of the Carrow community. They would also have read articles about what was being done back in 'Blighty':

Training the RAMC at Taverham
by Helen Colman

The colonel and other officers welcomed us most kindly when we reached the Park where the 3rd East Anglian Field Ambulance was in training. We learned that this consists, in war time, of 10 medical officers and 220 men, together with 58 horses and a large number of wagons.

Before describing our impressions of the visit, it is necessary to summarise the objects for which the Royal Army Medical Corps exists. It is maintained firstly, with a view to the prevention of disease (a most important branch of the work), every man being trained in all branches of military sanitary science, and secondly for the care and treatment of the sick and wounded ...

The first thing we were shown was the identity mark that every soldier has to wear hung round his neck, a metal disc about the size of a penny, only lighter in weight, on which is stamped his name, number, regiment, and the religious body to which he belongs.

Next, there was the small packet, at a guess about seven inches by four in size, containing first aid requisites – bandages, gauze and safety pins – which every soldier has to carry sewn into his coat, ready for immediate use.

When an action is expected it is one of the last duties of the officer in command, we were told to see that every soldier bears his identity mark and first-aid packet on him. These brought home to one the grimness of war.

Then we were shown a ground plan, drawn on paper, giving us the lie of the land. The Red Cross enclosure was to be so many yards in length and breadth. Here was the firing line, there was the part where the stretchers were brought with the wounded, at this end of the line were placed the most serious cases, that was the emergency hospital tent, and so on.

Stretcher Drill was the next item. Four men are told off to each stretcher (made of wooden poles and canvas), and they are sent to pick up the wounded. They have to search not only in the open, but in any brushwood there may be, for it seems to be the instinct of men as well as animals to seek to get under cover when wounded. One of the bearers carries a small, compact, knapsack-looking case containing an emergency outfit of first-aid resources. These panniers, we are told, show considerable improvement of those used in earlier campaigns. Various improvements since the Boer War were pointed out. Glass tubes and bottles – liable to breakage – had given place to black vulcanite, which has the added advantage of being lighter in weight. Compressed dressings mean a distinct gain in the space required for them. To us the cases seemed models of what such things should be. The golden rule observed in packing away things on a small boat was here carried out – a place for everything, and everything in its place, and not one half-inch to be lost …

The bearers came back from their search bringing the apparently-wounded, neatly bandaged. These bearers were then receiving daily training from the officers of the Medical Corps. Question and answer came promptly. 'What is wrong here?' 'Injured head, sir'. 'And this one?' 'Broken leg, sir.' 'What did you use a as a splint?' – And so on. It all looked very real to us, but happily the faces of the patients reminded us it was only what the children call 'make believe'. The stretcher-bearers are taught to make the best use of everything, and shown how a branch off a tree, a rifle, or anything that lies handy can be utilized to ease the pain and peril of moving the wounded.

Order and method seemed to mark every stage. Each wounded man had a paper ticket, torn out of a book, fastened on some button of his regimentals. On this was filed in his name, nature of wounds, and other details. Those who were seriously wounded had tickets with a red border, and as the stretchers were brought back, and deposited on the ground, they were placed so that the doctors could at once distinguish the serious from the slight cases, and know to whom to give the first attention. The stretchers were brought quite close to the Dressing Station, as it is technically called, which is really a tent rigged up as an emergency hospital. From there the patients are drifted off to a Field Hospital further from the firing line, or to a Base Hospital.

The Field Hospital which we saw was being utilized for a few patients requiring treatment for minor ailments. One was bathing his feet in some lotion. Patches of the skin were stained a bright turquoise blue, and I realised then why the request had gone forth that socks for the troops should be knitted in natural-coloured wool only. This case of poisoning from a coloured dye proved quite a troublesome one for a week or two afterwards, when going round the tents at the Norfolk and Norwich Hospital prepared for the reception of soldiers, I recognised this same man as a patient, still off being duty, and having been sent there to complete his recovery.

Attached to the Field Hospital was a Dispensary. The Dispenser, clean as a new pin in his white coat, was most anxious to show us all his appliances. He gave one the impression of alertness, efficiency and sympathy – just the quality most needed on a battle-field. I was sorry I did not know till afterwards that, though he had lately been at work in London, he was a native of Norwich.

One word before I close about the water cart for disinfecting water – however impure that may be. It was divided into two duplicate compartments, so that if one required cleaning the other still could be used. The water was forced in by a hand pump. It passed through a pipe, protected by a wire-casing intended to keep out 'leaves, or frogs, or such-like articles'. Then it passed through four sponges, which acted as a barrier to many impurities, and which required to be boiled periodically in order to make them clean again. Then there were four cylinders (technically called 'candles' if I mistake not), made of slightly porous earthenware, through which no known germ of disease can pass. The water is forced through these, and so the water which may enter the cart dirty and contaminated comes out clean and pure. We were also told of special disinfecting tabloids, used for purifying water when it is needed in large quantities.

The Wounded in our Norwich Hospitals
by Agnes W. Glen

Regarding our old city we might quote and say, that she is 'as full of memories as the Heaven is full of stars, and almost as bright', but amongst all the memories of the past surely few sights have touched the imagination of the people more tenderly than the first Convoy of wounded that came into our City from the great war.

For many weeks our hearts had been stirred with dismay at the thought of the sufferings of our soldiers in France and Belgium, and when an evening came and it was known that a little company of Red Cross workers were waiting for the first Hospital train, then hearts were thrilled as the words passed on from one to another through the streets – 'They are waiting for the wounded'.

And when the long procession of cars began and injured men were seen in all their dishevelment, then cheers of sympathy were raised and many a silent prayer was uttered – 'Use me too, oh Lord, even me, in this hour of national sacrifice'.

Soon the soldiers reached the Hospital, where skilled hands were waiting to minister to their many needs and where, before very long, they gladly found themselves in bed and within 'the cool kindliness of sheets'.

And now this scene has been gone through many times till it has almost ceased to stir the heart of the onlookers. For to the Norfolk and Norwich Hospital and to the Lakenham Military Hospital have come during the past months 2760 men. [She is writing in July 1915].

Usually a Convoy arrives late in the evening or during the night, and next day the wards are very quiet. The men who can are sleeping heavily from pure exhaustion, and doctors and nurses are moving silently behind screened beds, dressing wounds or preparing urgent cases for operation.

It is a sad sight, surely, this first day in hospital, to look down the long line of beds and see the many heads thrown back against the white pillows. Some of the men are young with the dew of youth still on their faces. Others look strong and rugged as if they had soldiered under many suns. All of them bear the marks of pain, or exhaustion, for these men have had stern work to do. They have been through the very gates of Hell itself. They have been made sacrifices for us against the evil in the world.

Many of them will get well and rejoin their regiments, but for others there remains only the long wearing pain, 'that makes of life one weary avenue of darkened days'. The worst pain does not always come from the most dreadful looking wounds, but often from some hidden tortured nerves that crucify the very soul and wring from the lips the cry – 'Would God it were morning,' and when morning comes, 'Would God it were evening.'

Sandbags for the Trenches

Among those connected with Carrow who have been connected with making sandbags for use in the trenches in France are various members of the Women's First-Day School, with help from Mrs Southgate and Mrs Emms, and many of the girls employed at Carrow during their dinner hour, superintended by Miss Clow, Miss Cox and Mrs Emms. Some of these bags have been sent to Lieut Cozens-Hardy, and some to Miss Tyler (the sister of a General at the Front), who has been appealing for them in *The Times*.

Miss Tyler writes: It is doubtful whether anyone, not actually in the Field, at all realises what the word sandbag means to the soldier in the firing line, or how urgently millions, and yet more millions, of sandbags are needed to stem the casualty lists.

The mother of a Captain in the Royal Field Artillery writes: 'I have sent my son 350 sandbags. He is delighted with them, and says his observation post has been safe for the first time since the last shift.'

An Infantry Lieutenant writes: 'We want a tremendous amount of sandbags … If your saw a shell burst on a parapet with sandbags, and on one without, you would soon see how many lives they save.'

A Captain, Royal Field Artillery, describes the way in which the infantry advance: 'Each man takes ten empty bags under his arm as he runs out. When fired at he drops, and fills a bag as he lies, for cover, then he dashes on again and again; always leaving the filled bag to cover some

A traditional image of a girl sitting at home dreaming of her soldier. (ACC 2013/320)

man behind him. In this way the whole line advances, with temporary cover, till they can dig themselves in.'

The following are the directions for making sandbags: They should be made of Jute Hessian. They must not be heavy, but strong, to stand wet and weight. They must measure when complete 33 inches by 14 inches. One inch turning seams, which must be strongly oversewn with double thread, or finely strong string; or machined with thread, two rows of stitching close together; not chain stitch. Mouth of bag to be left open and a piece of stout string two feet long must be tied on, three inches below mouth, ready to close the bag when filled.

The occasional article described some aspect of life on the front line:

The Ration Party
by 2nd Lieutenant S. W. Robinson, July 1917

The night previous we were relieved. A weary task which ended at 4 am, and we were fairly fatigued after four days' tour of duty in trenches three feet deep in soft clayey mud and water. Therefore we comfortably anticipated a good night's sleep in the support trenches.

Alas, for the desires of man! About dusk a runner came along to the dug-out with a chit (chits are bits of paper and more trouble than the Bosch) from Headquarters. 'One officer and twenty other ranks to report at the Dump at ----- o'clock as Ration Party to B Company.' I am detailed. I grin, pathetic and wan!

My party assembles in the trench. I explain what has to be done, emphasising the joy of ration carrying, and we start off for the Dump. It is rapidly growing dark, and as walking in the communication trench is exceedingly tedious, exhausting in fact, we clamber out and progress across that indescribable area, usually called 'over the top', so disfigured and torn, until we reach the road! Save the mark. It *had* been one of those long fine straight roads, lined by tall trees, which are a feature of France. Artillery fire had changed its aspect and shape somewhat. The trees were splintered and lying across it – 'twas as though some frenzied giant hand had torn them up and thrown them about haphazard. Yet its usefulness was not dead – it still served as a guide. And in that line our fellows are shivering and freezing at their posts. Their thoughts are with us, for rations mean warmth and comfort with which to combat the gnawing cold and saturating mud. We reach the Dump, find our wagons, and each man shoulders his burden of food, drink, fuel or mail.

Then the walk up to the Front. We do it in file, carefully picking our way in the dark, avoiding shell holes and small craters, stepping over trees, phone wires, and crossing crazy bridges over old and disused trenches. As we approach nearer and nearer we halt, and stand stock still on the burst of each Very Light, for who knows how many pairs of Hun eyes are watching for movement which, if spotted, is fired on at once!

As it is, the Bosch has the road, which had recently been his, registered, and periodical bursts of machine gun fire keep us alert – anon we hear the patter of bullets falling near to us and the crack of a sniper's rifle, but we are blessed by the gods and not a man is hit.

We leave the road at a point, and cut across to the right where lies our goal. Following a tortuous track we are careful not to lose we finally come to a trench. My party lies down. I flop into the trench and sink to my knees, then scramble to a glimmer of light – the Headquarters of B Company. Down thirty feet I find the OC [Officer in Charge] in his dug-out, to whom I report, hand over my rations, glean the news of the day, wish them good luck and good night, then I rejoin my party.

Just before we reach the road on the way back the Hun has a mild strafe and drops some high explosive on to it. Poor beaten thing, its scarred and shattered surface seems incapable of further destruction. We formed a curious affection for this bleeding stretch of earth – was it not an unfailing guide when we otherwise would be lost? So we crouch in shell holes watching, waiting and wondering until all is quiet again and we can resume our journey.

Back with our Company I find we are not required further, so we dismiss to our quarters and settle down for the night – at least until some pestilential chit calls for a working party!

The men would also have seen a roll of honour in every issue of the magazine, with the names of those who had been killed in action. Inevitably, officers were given more attention than private soldiers, as in these two examples describing the deaths of two junior officers:

Roll of Honour: It is with deep regret that we record the death of Second-Lieutenant Cuthbert Lawrence Richmond of the 5th Battalion, Northumberland fusiliers, who was killed in action on May 25th [1915].

Mr S J Woodcock, manager of the representative Staff, sends us the following particulars: Mr Richmond, who was in his twenty-sixth year, was the youngest son of Mr and Mrs R. F.

Preparing for the mud of Flanders on the fields in Norfolk. (MC 2283/1)

Richmond, The Laurels, Belaugh, Norfolk; he was educated at St Dunstan's College, Catford, and joined the Cannon Street Staff in January, 1906; he was attached to the Export Department until February 1914, when he was transferred to the Introducing Staff of the Company, and sent to Newcastle-on-Tyne.

On the outbreak of war, Mr Richmond tried to enlist, but as he had not then recovered from a serious illness, he was obliged to wait until December 12th before he was able to gratify his wish: he left for France on May 11th, being one of the many smart young Officers selected to replace casualties after the hard fighting of the first week in May. He was a man of fine presence and physique, genial and happy in his manner, and a general favourite. We offer our sincere sympathy to his sorrowing parents in their loss.

A pathetic interest will be felt in the following extract. It is from a letter received by Mr Woodcock just three days before Mr Richmond received his fatal wound: 'I must admit that when walking across the open to take over our trench, and heard bullets whizzing all around, I felt very squeamish and could not help ducking my head. It would make every Englishman's blood boil to see the utter desolation and ruin that have been caused here. Whole villages destroyed and burnt out, and the numerous little graves with their unpretentious graves dotted here and there over the fields, bear grim testimony to the awfulness of war'.

Second-Lieutenant W. F. Washington held a commission in the RAF. On 2 September 1918, he wrote a letter to Mr Aldrich of Colman's:

I came up to this squadron, which, by the way, is acknowledged as one of the finest in France, on August 2nd and started flying about the 4th. We were then up near the coast, and on a fairly quiet part of the front. I had a good opportunity to get thoroughly used to the height and method of flying out here, as I didn't get a scrap with a Hun for three weeks. The only exciting trip we did have was a fine squadron show, when we bombed a certain important railway centre about twenty-five miles over the line, from a height of 400 feet. That was some show I can assure you. And I am glad to say that every single machine, and there were over fifty, returned safely. We photographed the result, and the photographs, together with some prisoners' reports, showed that it was a tremendous success. The line was unable to be used for four days, and the stations, sidings and towns were horribly smashed up ...

About a week ago we shifted down south, right into the thick of the present push. I met my first Hun in this way. I was out on a single machine reconnaissance, and was just turning back for home, and five Huns' machines of a particular notorious character came down on me. I think I got one out of control, but I couldn't wait to see it crash as my front gun jammed and I had to fight a sort of rearguard action against the other four back to the lines. Luckily I got my machine and observer back safely. Well I don't want to meet five on my own another time, three are all right, but five is too many ...

We are having a pretty lively time at present. I shall be getting a fortnight's leave towards the end of October, when I hope to be able to come up and see you.

Washington never got his leave. Just one day after this letter was written, his machine was seen to fall in flames in the German lines. He and his observer were both killed.

Carrow Works Magazine was a symbol to its readers of the world for which they were risking their lives.

9

LETTERS HOME

Many Norfolk men serving on the Western Front wrote to family and friends at home describing their experiences of war. They varied from high-ranking officers to private soldiers. One of the officers was Jack Keir, a connection of the Upcher family of Sheringham Hall. He wrote a series of letters to his mother-in-law Fanny Simpson:

Croix du Bac, 5 November 1914:
The name of this place means the cross roads near the Ferry. Near here over the river Lys is the Bac St Maur or the ferry at St Maur. The Ferry is now a bridge and a very good one which the 6th Division took with small loss some days ago … I fear that we shall be here for some time but one can never tell and a sudden change may come. It seems quite certain that the Germans have failed in their attempt and will be depressed by their failure as they must recognise how serious their position is becoming. I am glad to hear today that more troops are coming out from home. This will enable some of the regiments who have been fighting so hard and who have had such terrible losses to have a rest. Up to the present our little army has had very hard work and altho the men are in excellent spirits both them their officers and staff require a certain amount of rest. We shall soon have 10 Divisions in the Field we ought to have at least 40! I don't suppose there has ever been a war in which the sick and wounded have received such humane treatment. As soon as a man is wounded and can be moved he is carried to the nearest Field Hospital where his wound is dressed. From thence he is taken in a motor ambulance to the railway where he is put into a hospital train and taken to a General Hospital and from thence to Paris or England.

   Col. Furse and I went to see the Indian Army Corps at their Head Quarters about 10 miles from here. They have naturally many difficulties to contend with but things are straightening out and I have no doubt that they will soon be well in order. I was very interested to hear about the men of the 6th Divn which they are looking after at Matlaske Hall. It is splendid the way people are caring for the wounded many of whom will be able to return to the Front with renewed health and vigour. Ethel will be quite a fluent French scholar by now. I wish I was. Our landlady still creeps in to enquire whether I am quite certain that the Germans will not return and take up their abode in her house. In spite of the fact that we do not always brush our boots on entering the house, and occasionally break one of her egg cups, we are still the favourites.

This is a most fertile country and even where shells are from time to time falling the men may be seen calmly ploughing the land. Every inch is cultivated and the absence of weeds would rejoice your heart. I visit my 4 Brigadiers (I have 3 of my own and a 4th, the 19th Brigade, attached to me at present) every day and it takes me about 3 hours and is a very pleasant ride as we go straight across country and have some small ditches to jump en route which breaks the monotony.

I must make a confession. This morning we had to fire at a church steeple from which a man was observing their artillery fire. About the 10th round we hit it at a range of about 5000 yards. Very creditable to the gunners. You must forgive them!

Christmas Day 1914:
Thank you for all your good wishes for Xmas and New Year. I do sincerely hope that 1915 may bring the blessing of peace to us all and prove one of the happiest in our history ... It froze last night and is freezing now so I have for the first time put on a pair of those nice undersocks you gave me to wear at Barningham. They do very well as they protect the soles of your feet and do not make your boots feel uncomfortable because your stockings are too thick and your boots too tight ... Last frost we had, several men suffered from frost bite. It is to be guarded against by not leaving them too long in the trenches, and by frequently changing their socks and rubbing their feet at the same time with mineral jelly, which contains, I fancy, paraffin in some form or other.

4 February 1915:
I am inspecting the Argyl [sic] and Sutherland Highlanders tomorrow and will look out for young Nicol in case he is in that battn. I have been asked to report on the young officers new in or have recently joined the service. At the conclusion of my inspection I shall have viewed about 300 young officers and about 16,000 pairs of boots. It is quite interesting seeing the different battalions and hearing the ideas of the different officers commanding and subordinate. They have now granted permission to a certain number of privates to go home on leave. It will a very much appreciated privilege. The River Lys has fallen several feet during the past few days and we are able to reoccupy several of the trenches from which we had been driven by the floods.

22 February 1915:
Thank you very much for your nice letter. I am indeed fortunate, as so many much more deserving men have not been allowed to reap the reward of their labours. General Gough, whose death is recorded today, is an instance. Young, capable and ambitious, he seemed to have everything before him. Had he been spared he was destined to fill some of the most important posts in our Army. When he was hit he was about 2000 yards from the trenches. A chance shot glanced off a road in front and passed thro' his body. A careful examination of his wound was made which tho' serious was not looked on as mortal. He is a brother of General Sir Hubert

Gough whose name was so prominent during the Ulster crisis. I feel certain that your and Alice's prayers on my behalf have not been unheard and can only hope that I may be spared to justify the confidence which has been reposed in me and to prove myself worthy of the honour my King and country has bestowed upon me.

7 June 1915:

There is just time to send you a few lines before dinner. Thank you for your nice letter of congratulations. I am very lucky to have got the command of a Corps but still more so to have got the command of such a good one. It is of course an added joy to have my dear 6th Divn under my command again. I shall of course endeavour not to favour them, but it will be very hard! My 3rd Divn has not joined me so far and I am not sorry as I am anxious to get to know the 4th before I go on to another one. Tonight we finish taking over a bit of the French line and I shall not be sorry as it is always good to know what you have to deal with and when you know your position is a secure one you need have no anxiety. Many thanks for the socks and shirts. My address remains nearly the same. Instead of Commanding 6th Divn it is Commanding 6th Corps.

I am sure it does the men a lot of good to be in such a beautiful place and among such cheerful surroundings.

9 July 1915:

Nearly every house round Ypres has the marks of shell holes in it and the Germans always shell a house they think we might occupy. It is a sad scene of devastation....All the care and kindness the men receive at the hospital must be very welcome to them. Most of them are all

The devastation at Ypres. (MC 947/1)

Dicklebusch, 1917. (MC 947/1)

the better for a change to England. They are going to give as many officers as they can a change home. The war has lasted so long that many of them are showing signs of the strain and require rest and change …

We have had some fighting here – on my birthday. We have been fighting with the Germans ever since. Today they have given in apparently and resigned to us a trench that we have been fighting for. Our Artillery has caused them many casualties.

13 September 1915:

We seem to have made up our minds that we shall be here this winter. All sorts of preparations to ensure our own and our men's comfort are being planned. Baths, drying rooms, wooden huts, stoves etc are in course of construction. When it rains we cannot get rid of water from the trenches and when we want water for our horses some way behind the firing lines, we have to dig 300 feet before we can get it! The men have for the time become gypsies and the life seems to suit them. Most of them have made their own beds which keep them well off the ground. We are not nearly so well off in the matter of houses as we were at Armentieres and so far all we can get are a few tents and some wooden huts. Before the winter comes I am sure we shall be better housed.

16 October 1915:

I have today been inspecting the 71st Bde, which now forms part of the 6th Divn. It consists of battalions of the Essex, Suffolk, Bedford and Norfolk regiments. The latter is the 9th and may have some men in it from your part. I talked to a very young sergeant who said he came from Norwich and was in the railway. He knew Barningham and had seen Walter there and at recruiting meetings. I had not time to speak to any of the men in the ranks of the Norfolks as I had 4 Battns to inspect and it took me all my time.

17 November 1915:

If all goes well I may be able to return home again for a week or ten days. I see you say that young Colman is in the 6th Corps, I suppose he is in the Norfolk Regiment. Alice wrote to me about a Major Langton a brother, or brother-in-law, of Mr Magnay who was at Sheringham. I went to see him yesterday.

Today I have had an interview with Sir John French: not a very trying ordeal. He was very pleasant and interviewed us one by one. It was like waiting to see the dentist …

21 December 1915:

I have been a long time answering your letter, but have put off, knowing you hear my news when Alice gets her letters. I am now taking the opportunity of sending you my best Xmas greetings and hope they will reach you in time. This is a regular typical Flanders winter day. Mild, slight rain and thick atmosphere. I stayed in this morning in hopes it might be clear by this afternoon. It is now 1.15 and there are no signs of fine weather so I fear the barometer must be set at 'set wet'. We had 3 ladies to dinner last night, Mrs Fenwick (Chaplain Roberts' sister), Miss Chomley (a cousin) and Madame de Glos, a very pretty and capable little woman. They are all nursing at the Belgian Hospital at La Panne and get leave occasionally to come over here to see that I am quite well…. They are very hard worked and have had nothing but night duty lately so sleep all day. Madame has a little house at La Panne so they all live there together.

Poor Dick Crofton my ADC returned with at least ½ a dozen parcels bigger than himself and a number of others. We eat [sic] some of his oysters last night and they were delicious. A surprise is being prepared for the children on Xmas Day. It is going to be quite a big thing. A tea and then "The Tree" followed by crackers etc and a distribution of presents. We are very proud of ourselves, at least I am very proud of my troops.

The Germans attempted a gas attack on us which entirely failed owing to the resolute bearing of our regiments who refused to yield to panic, stood their ground, and entirely disconcerted those abominable wretches who hoped to find us retiring in panic and disorder. It was a great achievement as now we have entire confidence in our gas helmets and are quite ready to meet these brutes on any terms. An ordinary attack on us is the one thing we long for but which the Bosch I do not think will dare to make. He would like to win Ypres as an advertisement. It has no other value.

Other officers kept diaries. One of the most laconic is that of Lord Wodehouse of the 23rd Division HQ, a typical entry reading,

7 January 1916:
General presented medal 69th. Rain. Heavies had chance of a lifetime on a big gun. Stuck in wad and ceased firing after 19.20.

Just occasionally an opinion creeps in:

8 March 1916:
Went to Chateau La Haie. Went to Ablain. Fine. How long shall we be here before we are shelled out.

The power of the tank is captured in this dramatic image – they were first used in battle in 1916. (MC 947/1)

Even the Battle of the Somme receives the briefest of mentions:

27 June: Vaux. Rain. Advance cancelled till Sat.

29 June: Vaux. Went to Hebatome. Bombardment. Dinner Amiens with John P.

1 July 1916: Intense bombardment 6.30. Attack 7.30. Watched from above Albert. Had tea Amiens. Moved forward evening.

However, he was sharp enough to note the key technological advance in the battle:

15 September 1916:
Offensive very successful. Tanks used for the first time. Courcelette. Martinpuich taken.

Wodehouse's modesty allows just this three word entry near the end of the diary:

3 January 1917:
Mentioned in Despatches.

Private soldiers naturally wrote letters which were less about the general picture of war and more about what they were personally going through.

One good example is found in the letters of William Ernest Capps of Gorleston. William was born in 1889, the son of William Capps, a chimney sweep, and his wife Clara. He had three brothers, Gus (Augustus), Richard and George ('Tross'), the youngest, and two sisters, Gerty (Gertrude) and Kathleen. Clara was a widow by 1911, and all the letters are addressed to 'My dear Mother'.

10 January 1916:
Just a few [lines] in answer to your nice letter, hoping to find you all quite well at home, as it leaves me in the best of health and still having a good time. I have just been having a brew up with the cocoa you sent, on the old camp fire. I have not received Ethel's parcel yet, I expect that have gone west. Well I must not grumble as I have been pretty lucky with my parcels and letters … I see by the papers that the butchers were all shut up in London one day, so things begin to look a bit fishy. Well if that go on like that, people will soon get fed up. I see my photo, that is better than I thought would be, as he had to take them twice the second time, 'I tell you they cannot get a glass strong enough for me'. Well I think I have said about all this time. With much love and best wishes to all.

(Roll on Peace. I don't think it will be long.)

Tipperary [undated]:
Just a few lines hoping this will find you all quite well, and it leaves me the best, but it is rather warm this part of the globe. If we have much weather like this, I shall soon melt all away. Well you see I have found Tipperary alright, there is a little truth in the song. I have got right down in the south of Ireland. I got on alright when I got to London, I was soon put on the right

road, but if I known then what I know now, I might have had another four or five hours at home instead of waiting in London. I will just tell you the hours it took. Yarmouth to London 5 hours, Euston to Holyhead 4½ hours, Holyhead to Dublin 3 hours, Dublin to Tipperary 6 hours. So you see there is not much chance of getting a weekend, as it spoils the look of two days travelling. We are camped just outside of Tip, the town itself is not a bad size place, but the chaps tell me that is not up to much walking about alone, so they have to go out in fours or half dozens, as some of the people do not think very much of us, but they are not all alike. You ought to see the damage done in Dublin by some of the rioters, I would not have believed it, if I had not seen it myself. Great buildings burnt, and pull down, they much have played the devil up there, by the look of tricks.

Tipperary [undated]:
We are having some grand weather at Tipperary, but we can do with a drop of rain, or else the corps [sic: crops] will soon be dried up. Well I am having pretty easy time of it, like a recruit again, just go for a little march during the day, and a little phisical drill and then we are done for the day. The grub here is pretty good, the Irish people are not on rations, only for sugar, but the price of food is very dear. Well I have had a look round Tipperary and the place is not so bad. Four of us went to the pictures the other night and they were pretty good, tell Tross I saw Charlie Chaplin there.

France [undated]:
We have shifted again since I wrote to you last, we have had a march and a long train ride just lately, we are sleeping at a fare size place now. I carry plenty of company about with me, which are known as chats, that is the name the Tommies give them, we generally have a hunt once a day [second page of this letter is lost].

France, 25 April 1917:
I see by your letter you had plenty of snow at Easter, and so did we this part of the globe. I see boy George is getting on now, from a halfpenny a week to a halfcrown, that is a good jump, so the old boy is in the barbering trade. 'Hay' you must tell him to mind he does not cut the people's heads off. Well I see food stuff is getting a nice price in England, fancy swede being fourpence and sixpence each, and potatoes are a nice price too, I suppose you will not get any at all directly, as they will be so dear for poor people to buy. Well mother I should like to being seeing to finish of this rotten war. I am getting fed up, and I do not know who isn't. I lost all my kit the last time up the line, I suppose the Germans had the contents, I do not mind that, as long as they did not get me.

Soldiers who were taken prisoner wrote back letters that showed how much they valued news from home:

My dear Mother,
At last I am able to write you a few more lines to let you know that I am quite well. Am sure that you wonder how I am faring. [lines crossed through by censor] waiting for the time to pack up for Blighty. I hope that you have received my postcards and letters and sent on some cigs. My address now is permanent.

How are all at home, I do want to hear but shall not get a letter yet I suppose, but keep up heart as I am alright and things will come right in the end. Cannot write more this week.

With best love to all.

My dear Mother,

I am more than glad to say I received two letters yesterday dated 21st and 24th June, one from Frances and one from Miss Ranson. I was disappointed not having one from you, but expect to get one this week as now they have started to arrive. I'm sure there are heaps waiting for me somewhere and will get them in time to read them. Yesterday was like starting in the middle of a serial [word illegible] not having read those previously sent. Frances tells me Father is under the Dr and cannot get up & in the middle of the hay making. I do hope that he is better as everything gets muddled up without him & its extra work for you. I feel worried about it & hope it will not be for long. I also gather from her letter that Hugh is expecting to come to England shortly.

Men who were too old to serve might go to France with the Church Army, an organisation dedicated to supplying refreshment – physical and spiritual – to soldiers behind the front line. One man who did this was William Hewetson, the vicar of Salhouse, whose whole family played its part in the war, as we have seen; his son Philip served in France, while his daughter Ruth worked in a Wiltshire Hospital:

Postmarked 29 October 1917:

My dearest dearest Kathleen,

Here I am at what you might call a half-way house, sleeping and eating at the Officers' Mess in the town, and with no duties and no home. No bags at hand. But if the majority of hours are spent killing time I have had some interesting experiences and talks. It is also unfortunate that the Hut is practically closed. The man in charge went yesterday to open a new Hut nearer the line. My old Hut was to have been moved and therefore nine days ago was shut. Then the military authorities had a new one put up with the result that mine now looks most uncared for, Mr E Phillips wanted me to go there till my exchange is arranged and I went up with all my bags etc. When I looked round I found no bed and blankets and generally an impossibility of work for a few days. I came back to the centre and reported progress or rather lack of it. When I first arrived no-one was here and then I find that until my new destination is settled we cannot send my passport to the APM and before I move it has to go to the new Army and back before I move away from here. One has to be prepared for much, but I could not have had a much worse start, and if it had not been for the first 5 months and knowing what can be done I should have been low indeed. My night journey was not at all bad really and my companion, a civilian doctor now a Lt-Colonel, gave me a most interesting account of his life (including courtship, marriage etc) and we got through the time well. Here I am not exactly in my element, but at dinner last night I had 2 companions at my table, and I had a most interesting and profitable conversation, and though of course we did not talk religion we were nearly all the time looking at life from the right and sound point of view, and I am thankful for the opportunities the meal offered. I drank their wine, smoked their cigarettes and have a warm invitation to visit their Mess if ever near them. Still I long to be settled though all this may be good for me. There have been many changes in personnel since I was here. I shall not be surprised if I have to wait for news but glad to get it when it comes.

5 November 1917:
One day about 10 men, more or less mud-logged, on their way to Hospital came in. The mud had made them more than tired; and this week I have had several instances. Imagine what it is, men with feet swollen from the mud yet having to tramp, with full kit, on hard yet sticky roads, many miles. They want more than a 'pub'. We give them the C.A. Recreation.

I served this week not a few officers in the canteen, but I do wish that more of the officers knew the life of the Hut as it is in full swing. During the summer I came across many officers who spoke openly of the value of the Hut to the morale of the men, but all do not because they never come in it.

Saturday 17 November 1917:
At last I have arrived at a new destination, but I am not sure whether it is likely to be a permanent one. To start with you need not send me my pillow or eiderdown as I shall be sleeping in a bed in a house, where the previous Superintendent lived. It is not quite ideal however, as the place is 7 or 8 minutes walk away, and I have all my meals at the Hut, where there is no separate place for the Superintendent. But I am trying to persuade the authorities to get an Armstrong Hut, which would be much better. I am quite close to the town where I wanted to be and in the wagon and horse lines of P's division, and nearly all the men in the Hut wear the mark which he does. It is a very nicely ordered Hut, with a very good orderly. Also there is a chapel to hold quite a fair number, which, however, seems to be used only for Holy Communion. There is a Chaplain too who lives quite close, who really seems able to do much of the work there is to do, and who takes an interest in the Hut so that my present idea (I have only been here 2 or 3 hours) is that I might well go where there is more scope, but I shall be glad to hear what P's movements are likely to be. If he comes out soon I do not wish too easily to move from the exact place where I am likely to meet him. It will probably be a few days before I get letters as my notice of new address could only go in the morning for any letters to be forwarded. Please remember APO S51. I sent a pc to you with that on it this morning. I travelled down here yesterday. After about an hour I changed and was then told that there was no other train that day. But then a French Leave train was mentioned and of course I could travel by that. It was all full of *poilus* in their blue costumes. However I got into a compartment nearly empty, which however swiftly filled up, and before I got here, though I could not talk to them, my cigarette case was empty too. Then I found C[hurch] A[rmy] Headquarters 20 minutes walk away, and had to leave all my baggage. I had understood a message had been sent through as to the day of my travelling, but the Commissioner was not at his Office nor at his diggings and when at last we met he said he had not expected me evidently for some days. Consequently no plans really had been made for me, a vague kind of idea that I was going to a Hut now building. However he took me to his room for a meal and after finding a bed for the night, which took some time, I was settled for the night. This morning he was off early, so that after a breakfast in an eating house, and a walk about the town, which included a shave, I walked out here in about 20 minutes, and later the Commissioner came round and brought my baggage in his car. It is of course a very much quieter spot than my previous Hut. It is a better planned Hut in many ways and

well kept. We are in a village quite close to a Church. I do not hear so much of the guns as I have been hearing, but they are there in the distance. The young Chaplain here seems a very decent chap, though actually only out here about a month. His name is Spread and his brother has been for 14 years in the Lancashires but owing to wounds is in England and now doing staff work, so P may know of him. I think his brother said he is a Major but now doing Staff Captain's work. I shall probably see a good deal of this Padre while I am here.

As I posted a letter to you yesterday I do not think there is much more news to be given. Description of places being forbidden, and that of persons being unwise. It has already struck me how much more necessary is the French tongue than in the parts I have left. Here English is of very little use and the French vocabulary is practically necessary, and I expect that willy nilly I shall have to try and talk.

Sunday 18 November 1917:
As soon as I arrived here I sent a note to Ruth and also to Philip, I sent my address which I was surprised to find allowed the name of my destination to be given. However, there it is. Matters will gradually shape out here, but at present I am rather lost. This morning I walked to a near C[asualty] C[learing] S[tation], and fortunately found a service at 11 with H[oly] C[ommunion] following, and made the acquaintance of the Padre, with whom I go to breakfast tomorrow, and on to a meeting of Padres, and I shall hope there to get into touch with the authorities to help me in getting necessaries for the Hut, as it is I believe at HQ where such-like people live. Starting a new work there are so many things to get that one rather takes for granted in life. None of them can you get except through Army, some of them Army will give, some of them it will allow you have on filling up forms on repayment. But it all means going to HQ (some official or other) and it takes time finding out who is the right person for each article. Most of the furniture is to come from the town I have left, by lorry, and until it comes I cannot do much, except to get to know the lie of the land, which gradually I am doing. I have bought all the stuff necessary to start the canteen, but not such a varied stock as I shall hope to have later on. Sugar will, I fear, be a great difficulty, I mean for the canteen. Neither sugar nor candle could I buy yesterday, but I mean to try some other GFC the next day or two. The GFC I go to is in a village barely 20 minutes walk away from here. One of my mess mates here has control over some 20 steam lorries so he provided me with one to bring all my goods home. I started with about 6 cases of biscuits, one of chocolate, 1 of condensed milk, one of Woodbines in packets, about 450 tins of cigarettes, 5 gross matches and a few smaller items. Then I hope for other goods from the CA stores.

9.30 pm: My two huts quarrelled this morning and have separated. The amusing part is that the one who remains goes on 2-day leave tomorrow and I am left alone. I was out all aft[ernoon] with the other. Later I shall be able to write more. We went to call on the general who is taking a personal interest in the Hut. He was out, but I expect him round in a day or two, and hope to get all done that is necessary. We had tea on the way back with officers of a Labour company. I saw those of another company yesterday.

I meant to have written a long letter, but the 2 men have taken up all my time.

Monday 19 November 1917:
I am now having another period of waiting for home letters till my new address gets through. Life will probably have more interest however than latterly. My two erstwhile companions,

Church and cemetery, Reninghelst. (MC 947/1)

The fall of Bapaume. (MC947/1)

men of 52 and 48, are both wealthy men. One, a colonial, Australian, v large sheep farmer (70,000 sheep) with many relations high in the army, who at any rate wrote once direct to HQ of all for favours wanted; the other rather a difficult self-indulgent Englishman, rich manufacturer I should think, no I think he said he was a barrister but with never a brief, a Marlburian. Well, tonight I have had dinner alone, soup, pheasant with potatoes, and pears and apples (fruit). And, if I wanted it, whisky, soda, port wine. Still I look forward to getting settled into the Hut at an early date.

This morning was quite interesting. First of all I breakfasted with the Chaplain in his Mess, then we motored in the dentist's car to our place of meting, where we first of all had a stroll onto a ridge which is really an extension (a spur) of the famous ridge taken early in the year by the Canadians. Every yard of the ground practically is indented by shell holes, barbed wire everywhere, trenches all more or less demolished, but all still in existence, a large crater the result of a mine, and the place of our meeting was a town possibly the size of Thame originally, not a house or cottage inhabited or habitable, the majority levelled almost to the ground and the rest looking like they would tumble at a touch. The whole district devastated in a way too sad to describe. Then you see everywhere cemeteries, all nicely cared for, and occasionally you get a single cross where evidently it had not been possible to carry the brave warrior to rest amongst other comrades, but just as reverently laid to rest and the place marked. I suppose here, being on the ground over which our troops have advanced, leads to this difference in the landscape from what I have been accustomed to, but it is sad to see now the trees blasted and without life, most of them just stumps about 20 feet high and not one with a sign of life …

I shall be glad of some refills for my flashlight if Ruth can remember the size, I told her. I should think there is scarcely any greater need out here for the winter than a flashlight. My CCS chaplain told me he came a cropper the other day and I had a nasty fall last night, suddenly going down a bank on the top of which I was standing, bruising my back against a stone. The result is now passing off but it made it quite difficult to move for a time. We had been out longer than expected and were caught by the darkness. I shall be quite right now from the fall, but I do not want to be without my light these dark nights. I am trying to get a good one out here, but am not sure whether I can, as it is through Army. Nevertheless I mean to try.

To Ruth, 15 January 1918:
As to yourself, there was before the war a great deal, and there is still now something to be said for the Varsity education for girls but I do not think that for general life girls need the 'Life' so much as men. With them it will always be education, and the result of education possibilities of future work, though the Oxford life must produce the same kind of effect as it does on men. But as I say I do not think it is so necessary as it was before the war. Then it was polish, the polish of the varsity life that was valued, now it is going to be far more 'Living Men and Women' … This is life now out here. Those who cannot come out here can enter into it at home, but many do not. You would most thoroughly appreciate value and enter into the Varsity life and all that even Oxford in all its marvellous life can give, and give perhaps better than any place in the world, but yet I am glad I think to know that you are feeling even more just now the call of Life … It needs just now girls who can give and who are willing to give of their very best, girls that are fitted by nature and by providence to be leaders in this

new world, where quite apart from politics, but including them, women will be able to give the purest, simplest influence, and a gentle wise influence in building up the new natural life.

I cannot express any opinion on the particular work that you write about now, but it is plainly a body in which you could influence for good for strength and wisdom ... and would be doing a national work of really great importance. Of course the drawback is leaving Mother at the present time, especially if both P[hilip] and myself are in France.

To Ruth, 13 February 1918:
I wish for many reasons that they had seen fit to give you a Commission, but if it is simply on the score of age, there will be plenty of girls of your new position in life and of like sympathies with yourself in the same position. And then surely most of the girls who go in for this kind of work that you will be doing will be girls with the same kind of desire to use their [talents] for their country and for their fellow countrymen. And amongst them all you are sure to find many religiously minded girls, though on going out into the world you are sure to find some just the opposite, some brutish and some weak and easily led. But I am sure you must be just bubbling over with desire to taste this new life, and I trust it will be work that you will thoroughly enjoy, and be able to see the usefulness of the work that you have to do, for it is sure to have its drudgery side. Out here I think that everyone is apt to question at times: Of what use is this work that I am doing? Could I not do better work elsewhere? After those times when I have done practically nothing at all except sell at the counter I have been tempted to ask these questions, but still I have realised more than ever that religion is living more than talking. And that it is the willingness to do anything and everything which will tell with the men now and afterwards. We are just cogs in a great wheel, but the engine needs every cog to be in its place and running smoothly.

Soldiers also wrote to local newspapers describing their experiences. A man from Dereham, known only as Allen (his surname) wrote to the *Holt Post* in June 1917 with this vivid description:

At eleven o'clock Thursday night the ---------- Division marched to the front line trench, facing the town of ----------- held by the Germans. At 7.30 the following evening our division was to go over the top and take the town at all costs. I could not sleep during Friday morning. I however awoke about three o'clock Friday afternoon and could not rest after that. The hours and minutes dragged on – six o'clock everyone was restless – my thoughts flew to Dereham.

7.15: I lit one of your Army Club cigarettes, but after having two or three draws I threw it down. I could not keep still.

7.25: how slow the seconds seemed to go. Somebody said, 'Three minutes to go, boys'. Good God, I must pull myself together. I whipped out my bayonet and fixed same, and also examined my rifle. Two minutes to go, my brain was in a whirl. Every incident in my life came before me in the next two minutes. Hark! The greatest barrage fire or bombardment ever known in history had begun. The batteries of many divisions were bombarding the German position. It was 7.30.

I grabbed my rifle and bag of bombs and clambered over the parapet. All was confusion. The smoke from tens of thousands of our shells had made it impossible to see. Halloa!

Several of our men were going down, we were advancing too quick. Twenty-eight minute to eight. That's better. The barrage had lifted 200 yards. A Company's officer was yelling, 'Lead on, A Company'. We came down to the guard position and made one mad rush. Men were falling all around me, but I still kept on! Ah! We had reached our destination at last! A party of German bombers put up a bit of a fight and wounded four or five of our men, but seeing the number of us with fixed bayonets they surrendered. The rest of the battalion rushed on right through the town. My platoon had previously had orders to stay in the village or town, and bomb the dug-outs whilst the remainder dug a trench on the other side of the town …

Allen threw a grenade down a dugout as ordered; forty-four Germans came out with their hands up. As German shelling was heavy, the men of the platoon took shelter in a German-built dugout:

On arriving at the dug-out we at once made our way down the steps. They seemed to be an everlasting flight of steps. Eventually we reached the bottom. Then there was a little corner: we turned the corner. Good heavens! Look at this! Heydon Hall wasn't in it! There before us was a huge wonderfully constructed tunnel nearly as long as Dereham Corn Hall, and about 20 to 30 feet wide.

I sank down into a very comfortable arm chair. Beside me was a nice little table laden with good things. I opened a box and lit up a cigar, and I might add German cigars are A1. Easy chairs, tables, beds, beautiful stove and oven for cooking, to say nothing of tinned meats, cigarettes, figs, bottles of wine and enough bread to open a baker's shop.

Eventually Allen's platoon had a message to join the rest of the men, who had advanced 300 or 400 yards the other side of the village:

The shelling had quieted down a bit, so we made a bolt for it, and after several more exciting experiences reached the Blue Line about 3.30 the following morning to find the cookers, splendid rum issue, oranges, figs, dates, bread, cheese, pickles etc, waiting for us. In fact there were rations for nearly 1,000 men, but they were not all there to eat them.

10

A WORLD WAR:
GHURKAS AND CHINESE

The war involved men from all over the world. Two Norfolk men have left accounts of their experiences with troops of other nations. Captain Arthur Neville-Rolfe was with the 5th Royal Gurkha Rifles; he was in India when war broke out, and went with his men to the Western Front. Roland Lestrange, too old for regular employment in the Army, found himself in charge of Chinese labourers in France.

Neville-Rolfe wrote,

Three days out of Karachi at ten o'clock at night we joined up with the Bombay convoy. It was a wonderful sight for there were no enemy submarines and all the ships were fully lit with morse lamps twinkling everywhere. The sorting out of some 60 ships went quite smoothly and, as the Persian Gulf and East African convoys moved off north and south, we were reformed into three lines ahead, some thirteen ships in each line, and made for Egypt and France. It was extremely hot in the Arabian and Red Seas and of course it was the horses that felt it. The only ventilation that they got was through large canvas funnels let down through two open hatches and, as the pace of the convoy, was the pace of the slowest ship, not much air percolated down to the horse deck. The 17th Lancers officers and men were magnificent and would be down in the hold in shifts night and day. If a horse in the line collapsed it might mean that fourteen others had to be moved to get him out. He was then led round under the air shaft until he recovered. By then another would have collapsed and the whole process had to be repeated ...

After several days delay in the base camp at Marseilles I was sent up to the Front by a very roundabout route in charge of various drafts for the Indian divisions. We stopped frequently and were very soon hours behind our timetable. This meant that our scheduled cooking halts just disappeared. The drafts had been given no cooked rations and soon became extremely hungry. After vain expostulation to the guard I took matters into my own hands. At the next convenient stop I put sentries over the engine driver and got the men out into a pleasant countryside where they could cook a meal and enough food for anticipated delays to come.

A Gurkha soldier. (MC 2847)

My French is rather better than the usual public school conversational French but I did not need this to understand that the guard and I did not see eye to eye. I quite expected to hear more of this incident but I never did.

I joined the 2/8th Gurkhas who had been very badly knocked about and only had one British officer who had been through it from the beginning. On one occasion in particular half the battalion had suffered very severe casualties. They had taken over from a Highland regiment, as usual in the dark. When attacked at dawn many of the men could not use their rifles as the firing step was too low. In future reliefs every man carried a sandbag which he could fill if he required it ...

I am not going to describe the unpleasantness of that first winter in the trenches, but I must mention my primitive bombing course. On my arrival I was appointed battalion bombing officer and together with six Gurkhas was sent to learn the tricks. The only bombs then in use were the 'jampot' and 'hair-brush' varieties. The first was a tin jampot filled with slugs and high explosive, the second an enlarged lady's hair-brush with a slab of gun-cotton in place of the bristles. Both were detonated by a length of fuse which the thrower could cut to any length required. If he cut it too short the bomb exploded before it reached the German trench and if too long it was returned pretty quickly. All very tricky but after an hour's instructions we were all considered to be bomb experts. A subaltern's innings that first winter averaged a month and I didn't much overstep my quota. I was hit in the foot during an abortive night attack on some quite untenable trenches and was back in hospital at Osborne on Christmas Day.

When I was discharged from hospital in January 1915, I went down to my home in Norfolk to convalesce … Towards the end of January I was woken one night by what sounded like twenty motor cycles charging down a neighbouring hill, but proved to be the first Zeppelin raid on England. The airship, flying very low, crossed the coast at our village, giving Heacham the distinction of receiving the first bomb ever dropped on English soil. It was an incendiary and appropriately dropped into a washerwoman's soft water butt. What she said about 'Them there Germans' might have stopped the war had the Kaiser heard it. The second bomb was a 50 kilo H.E. which did not explode. It fell in a ploughed field near a chalk pit which was probably mistaken for a large house of importance. It was salvaged by the local sappers, and then displayed at the Yeomanry Mess as a nine days wonder.

By mid-February I was passed fit, and crossed the channel two days after the Germans had announced their intention to sink all ships without warning. The daily cross channel steamer crowded with reinforcements and officers, men returning from leave, would have been a great prize, but I don't think they ever got it. I was surprised that no precautions were taken except a complete black-out, and full steam ahead. I and a friend [Owen Gough, who was afterwards drowned in the P&O *Persia*] sat on a chest containing lifebelts, but I never saw a chest opened or anyone wearing a lifebelt.

The next big event was our first big offensive near Neuve Chapelle, the 2/8 Gurkhas being in divisional reserve. Gun ammunition had been so tightly rationed when I was out in 1914 that a twenty minute preliminary bombardment sounded quite phenomenal. We had started the war with very inadequate supplies of gun ammunition, and when trench warfare developed the emphasis was all on H.E. An H.E. bombardment is most impressive but I doubt whether it is as good as shrapnel for wire cutting. Be that as it may much of the German wire was uncut that day. My first duty was for my company to escort 400 German prisoners back to divisional headquarters, and we passed the Lahore division moving up to support the attack. I was suddenly hailed by Champain who had come out to the 1st Gurkhas. I think he recognised my pony Radium before me. The prisoners were confined in a three storey barn for the night, and I had to communicate with their senior officer in French as there was no one in the 400 who could talk English. The barn was not much of a prison for anyone determined to escape, so I made out my Gurkha company to be men of most ferocious habits who would use their kukris on the slightest provocation. However I think it was much more the morning's bombardment than my threats that enabled me to hand over my full quota of prisoners next morning.

When I got back I was briefed to take ammunition up to point X in the captured German trench system that night. Owing to a very inadequate plan of the trench system I had considerable difficulty in finding point X. In the past 36 hours the Germans had moved up both infantry and guns to block any further advance, and the ground behind our advanced line was being plastered in the hopes of catching parties of our men in the open. When I went up there again in the early hours with a second load, the shelling had slackened enabling me to take my party above ground for some of the way. I particularly remember the sweet smell of the German trenches – probably delousing powder – a smell I had already experienced in the barn the night before.

The battalion was occupying a redoubt behind our original line. Unfortunately directly behind us was a barn which proved a perfect mark for German gunners who wanted to register on the redoubt. We had been left alone until the third morning, and then the fun began. I was caught by one of the after breakfast salvoes of H.E's and it being before the days of tin hats, I was blooded as if I had been hit with a shot gun. Though very messy, it was mostly superficial except for a splinter that lodged between my eye and my brain – a souvenir that I still carry. That was the end of my second innings, this time several days before my scheduled quota of one month.

Roland LeStrange's diary:

Having pulled every rope I could for the last 3 months with the object of getting 'oven-ready', the War Office at last made a great favour of commissioning me to the Chinese Labour Corps, as from August 13 1917. They proposed I should start at a week's notice but as I politely refused to do this, they gave in (as I afterwards found out, being so hard up for 'Captains') and allowed me leave until September 7th.

On this eventful morn, had it not been for the kindness of Lord Churchill, in lending me his car, I don't know how I should ever have got 'off' from Victoria at 7.25 am. I had tried at numerous garages (and the station) the day before to get some conveyance, but quite failed.

Charlie came up from Henley the night before and was of great use in finishing off packing, and then saw me off from the station in the morning.

I only forgot one thing that I meant to take with me, but that gave me great sorrow, namely the pen (fountain) with which I am now scribbling, and which I am lost without.

When showing my warrant at the barrier, my duties began, as I was informed by the Rail Transport Officer that I was to be OC [officer in charge] train, and he gave me the names of 4 subalterns to work under me. Being naturally of a retiring disposition I did not appreciate this honour, especially as I was given no instructions as to what I was responsible for. I didn't see my way to stopping fellows jumping out, if they changed their minds, on the way down to Folkestone, and as soon as we had started I got hold of an attendant and told him to fetch one of my 4 subs, whichever he could come across, to review the situation.

At last I got hold of one, and he knew no more than I did, so I told him to take stock of me, as I should never know him again, and if there was any dirty work on at Folkestone, never to leave me!

The only instructions I had got, were to report myself to the Railway Transport Officer; so on arrival I at once did so (at about 9.30) and asked him what was my next move? To my relief he said all I had to do was present myself to the boat at 12 o'clock. The reason for this was that my train was only an officers' leave train, but had it contained troops, my hands would have been full as I should have had to march them 3 miles off to a Rest Camp for breakfast, and then have superintended their embarkation: a piece of luck anyhow.

On the train my first experience of robbery was perpetrated. I was charged 2/6 for travelling in the Restaurant Car! In France this sort of thing is normal as everyone is 'out' to make the English pay.

We had an excellent crossing, starting at 12.30, a fleet of 4 troop ships in all, escorted by 4 destroyers. The first sight of everyone in life-belts was novel, but they are far from comfortable as one cannot sit down and lean back in them and it's difficult to get at one's pockets. My particular boat was packed with troops, about 1500.

We arrived at Boulogne at 1.45 pm.

BOULOGNE

Before leaving England I had been instructed to proceed to Noyelles, the HQ of the Chinese Labour Corps, further I was given to understand that I should be in a billet. As a fact the authorities at home know as little about the labour management in France as the 'man in the moon'.

On landing, I at once made off to the RTO's office for instructions – I may here mention that as a rule RTO's are a surly, jacks-in-office class who treat one like dirt – and he told me that I was not to proceed to Noyelles, but that I was to report myself to the Assistant Military Landing Officer, who would instruct me what to do. This kind official told me to further report myself to the OC Labour Base Depot, at the Heuriville Camp. Some 1½ miles out, up the most infernal hill.

It cost me 6 francs to get there, with my luggage, in a fiacre and then for the first time it dawned on me that life in France meant under canvas, and here was I, with no Camp furniture or requisites, in fact nothing but a sleeping bag which I had providentially brought out.

I saw the Adjutant and explained him how I was situated, but he said the Colonel absolutely insisted on all officers sleeping in Camp, and that perhaps with a board or two I could make shift, as I should probably only be there a week or so!

I went off to the Quarter Master and requisitioned 5 blankets, with difficulty I got 5 pieces of board (incidentally full of nails) and with the aid of two beer boxes made some sort of a bed. The tent had no floor boards, and two other inhabitants not counting various specimens of the animal and insect kingdoms.

I never liked taking on any job less, and felt when I lay awake that night with my two 'ranker' stable companions snoring, that it was a year since I had left civilisation!

However, I survived it! Though it did last nearly a fortnight.

This Camp, as previously stated, is the Base Camp of all Labour Corps. There are 10,000 to 12,000 'troops' here comprising compounds of Egyptians, Chinese, English, Indians etc, besides prisoners of war and Officers' Training Corps. It overlooks the sea to the S.W. of the town, and is in charge of a Commandant. My immediate C.O. was one of the most ill conditioned fellows I ever met, one Lt-Col Shaw. I believe he was a Midland haberdasher, anyhow not a soldier, and with the manners of a wash house rat. When he came into the Mess hut he made everyone stand to attention, and if they did not do so 'dressed them down' in public. In fact I soon sized him up, and determined to get my 'oar in' with him, before he did with me! I found that I was one of only two Captains present, amongst 87 subalterns, with the result that I was 'Captain of the day' every other day. My duties were not really strenuous. 6 am Mess breakfasts and instruct Orderly Officers and Sergeants as to their duties. 8.45 parade officers. 1.50 pm parade officers. During day tour camp, turn out 2 Guards and visit the Detention Compound. After 11 pm turn out Guards again, and see all lights out by sunset.

The net result was that my afternoons were practically free. So on the 4th day of my sojourn at Heuriville, I reported at the CO's hut and asked (greatly to his surprise) if I could have a word with him. I said I felt highly honoured at being on duty every day, but if he had no objection I did not propose to adhere to the order that the Captain of the day was to remain in Camp during his term of duty.

That, when my work was finished, there was nothing on earth to do, and that a telephone message to Officer Club Boulogne would find me in case of trouble! He was so taken aback at being tackled by anyone that all he said was; Very well, Lestrange, I will tell the Adjutant – Good.

The 'Staff' as a fact were quite good fellows: Capt Richardson (2nd in command). Lt Stagg (Adjutant) and Lt Gerald C Hudson who draws weekly a military cartoon for "Sketch" and to whom I told a story or two which he illustrated.

My interview with the Colonel proved so effective that he was gracious enough to ask me to sit next to him at Mess the next night. I may mention that his table had entirely different food to the rest of us!

The damp here is awful. I pile my clothes on top of my 'luggage' (none of which I have opened, practically) and on getting up the next morning everything is saturated with wet. Matches left in the tent won't strike after 24 hours.

I think the most damnable discomfort of 'tent' life is the distance you may be off an 'E.C.' [earth closet]. I was singularly unfortunate in every case. At Heuriville it was quite 150 yards, and to take this journey in the dark, and in 'any old' weather that may be on hand, is enough to break one's heart. The one and only bath was at the same spot (with perhaps 50 competitors) but as oil was unprocurable to warm the water, it had little interest for me.

Now as to my brother officers, words must fail me to describe them properly. 99% of them have no pretensions to the designation of 'Gentlemen'. Many of them have been in prison (more ought to be!), half of them are drunk daily, as well as nightly, they have no knowledge of military etiquette or in fact manners of any sort. Their language and conversation I am sure beats the East End of London.

The reason is this (especially among the Chinese section): they have all been imported directly from China, where they have lived for many years without having returned to England. They are composed of miners, clerks, small prospectors, underling officials etc, whom, because they know a certain amount of Chinese, are commissioned as Second Lieutenants regardless of age or honesty!

Theft was rampant in the Camp, but as it is all a passing show, of here today and gone tomorrow, there is no chance of bringing matters home. (I should state that these remarks re drunkenness and theft apply to the Noyelles camp in particular.)

Here is an instance – by an old hand. With difficulty I had persuaded the Mess President to sell me a bottle of whiskey to take to my billet, the price of it in shops being prohibitive and at the Canteen you cannot buy less than a dozen. This I put in my overcoat pocket and hung it up amongst many others at the entrance to the Ante-Room. In a quarter of an hour it had gone! No-one but a brother officer could have taken it. I told my batman I would give 2 francs for the bottle, full or empty, if the tent orderly could find it. He did find it the following day – naturally empty – and wrapped up in a piece of paper and put into the Staff dustbin!

The roughest of the rough are the Newfoundlanders. I had one in my tent – he had an M.C. He slept in all his clothes, did no washing (except his hands), was shaved every other day in the town, and his ablutions in the morning consisted smoking a foul cigarette and spitting on the ground of the tent!

One night he never turned up at all, but arrived next morning at 6 o'clock. I suggested he was rather late (he being a Second Lieutenant and Temporary Captain) but all he remarked was 'I suppose I have a right to spend a night in the town if I like'. I told him, unfortunately I was Captain of the day and that I should have to report him. He took great exception to this (especially as a tent-mate of mine) but it was obviously impossible for me to do otherwise. He began to cry and say that my threat if carried out would ruin his chance of promotion and his career. In the end I begged the Adjutant to deal with the matter himself and not report it to the Commanding Officer as such behaviour could only be accounted for by discipline being an unknown quantity to him. A severe dressing down was all he got – but he was very lucky …

A few days after my arrival I was sent in charge of 20 officers to procure, from St Martin's Camp, 'tin hats' and anti-gas masks. We started at 1 o'clock and walked 1½ miles into the town, crossed it, through the Old Quarter, and up the most villainous hill 4 miles the other side of Boulogne. On arrival we found a company being put through their facing in 'Gas Drill' and we fell in them.

For 4 solid hours we were instructed how to put on and take off the masks in the shortest space of time. We were each supplied with a helmet, a 'Box' mask and an 'HP' helmet. This latter is really a sack you put over your head and tuck into your uniform and is only in case the 'Box' should go wrong (which has superseded it).

It was rather troublesome to me at first, owing to my false teeth, as one is supposed to grip the inhaling tube between the teeth, however I managed to get the same effect by shoving it down my throat. At the finish of one's preliminary instruction, we were invited to pass through an airtight hut 15 yards long containing the most offensive sulphurous smoke (which even outside nearly knocked one down where it leaked out) to see if the masks really fitted properly.

There was a typical looking village schoolmaster next to me (a brother officer) who was in a 'blue funk' of passing through the 'lethal chamber' and he made me laugh by turning to me and saying, 'If I had known I should have been subjected to this indignity, I should never have volunteered to come out here'. Considering he had then got his mask on all cock-eyed and looked even more comical than one usually does, it is not to be wondered I nearly choked myself and had to take off my own hangings to get fresh air.

As a result of it all, I went twice through the smoke ordeal with perfect comfort, so I shall feel some confidence if I have to use it in earnest in the future. Before leaving, and to complete the course, we formed up and had 3 different sorts of bombs exploded amongst us. By the row they make on exploding you can tell whether they are poisonous gas, explosive or incendiary bombs and act accordingly. After a week's further drilling on the beach at Le Portel where we had to march and double in this confounded head-gear, I succeeded in carrying out the desired result, namely, that the whole thing must be securely fixed on your head within 10 seconds of the alarm being given of 'Wind, dangerous'.

Just before I had arrived at Boulogne, they had had 3 days and nights running of bombing. Fortunately for me we only had 3 'scares', but these being at night, and I being on duty, they were most annoying. Naturally all lights are turned out and I had to grope my way, in the pitch dark, up and down the lines (and there were 16 rows of tents without including the officers' tents) stumbling over ropes and pegs and damning freely. The only really important thing to find, was the fire picket, but when after a long grope I ran into them, I found they were only 3 strong instead of 12! The disturbance was, in each case, over in under an hour, the aeroplanes apparently confining their attentions to Calais and Dunkirk.

At mid-day on Sept 15th a 'ZZ' Boat came close inshore opposite our Camp, and was detected by the land batteries. She was shot at from every direction but I am afraid got away un-injured. It was blowing half a gale and raining at intervals.

NOYELLES
After a hurried meal (?) we walked into Boulogne (about 12 of us) and started punctually for Noyelles via Etaples arriving at 4.30.

Noyelles is a little village of a few hundreds of inhabitants 5 or 6 miles from the mouth of the Somme. It contains 2 Chateaux, i.e. fair sized houses, one 'public' and one stores, which has also a "drinking and billiard saloon". It has a Mayor, who is the Censor, and is a young damsel also holding the position of Schoolmistress. The Chinese Camp is just outside the village.

On my arrival I found the same old condition of affairs as I had left at Heuriville. Tents, no bed boards, very crowded, 3 in a tent, no huts for even a mess and the Mess itself beggaring description.

A surprising feature in France is the length of the trains and the excellence of the permanent way from (in my experience) Boulogne to Amiens, and no doubt on to Paris and beyond. One day I counted the coaches and also stepped on. The coaches were 18 yards long and there were 50 of them. This would give a train of over half a mile in length! This is quite normal. Then as to the line itself. It runs between two little fences with very groggy looking telegraph posts parallel to it, it is all overgrown with weeds, no-one ever seems working on it, and yet it has carried for over 3 years all the heavy traffic, in the shape of guns and troops, of the war. I wonder what would have been on the LC&D or the GER!

I soon tumbled to it that I should never be able to carry on with satisfaction to myself, not to mention those over me, as a Company Commander. With the winter coming on, living under canvas, in some small village possibly just behind the Line, I could not foresee myself doing a week's good work. So I had several talks with Fairfax in which he quite agreed with me, and was prepared to allow me to try and get some other job. In the meantime he said he would not post me to a company, but that I could just carry on with the ordinary routine of camp life at HQ. [However, due to a shortage of captains plans were changed.]

I was posted by the Col to No. 99 Company on 22 October, and told I had to repair to Saingville in the course of a day or two. Saingville is about as lively a spot as you could wish to cast anchor at, anywhere short of close up to the Line.

It is close here, 2 or 3 kilometres from Abbeville where is one of the largest munition dumps in France. It is the one place the Huns are trying to hit off in this locality, but so far they have not quite got it. My Chinese labourers have the loading and unloading of munitions. It is situated in the middle of the marshes, for safety, and needless to say all are under Canvas. I at once took over the Command of the Corps (99) … but I went to bed that night feeling my prospects were not very 'rosy'!

I had just turned in when an orderly tapped at my door with a 'chit' from the Col saying it was all a 'wash-out' but that I was to proceed to Calais at 1 pm on the following day to take command of no. 70 Company. I went to sleep giving the whole thing up as a bad job!

THE CHINESE

A company consists of about 490 Chinese 16 white NCOs, 4 subs and a Commander. It is usually divided up into platoons of 100 strong with 2 Sergeants and 2 Corporals. The Company itself is divided into four 'Classes': Interpreters; Gangers; Dressers; Coolies.

To the Interpreter one has to turn for everything, and you are really in their hands. This is a great drawback as some of them are no better (honest) than they should be, with the result that what you wish expressed is not put properly before the Coolies and vice-versa. They are drawn from the "scholars" of China and are a head and shoulders above the rest. They would correspond to our Sergeant Majors.

The Chinese labourers' camp, with the tents being painted for camouflage. (LEST supplementary 39a)

The Gangers represent our NCO's and as such conduct all the supervision of work, for which they are responsible to the white Sergeants and Corporals. Lastly the Dressers are practically hospital orderlies, and as such command respect from the Coolies. It is possible that while I am writing this – as China has now come into the War – the method of dealing with them may be altered, but it must be understood that they are not a military force, and stringent regulations have been laid down by the War Office to the effect that they are not to be drilled, or any military terms made use of, in designating their ranks etc. Hence the word Ganger.

All this has been brought about politically and from the trouble that (politically) took place over 'Yellow Labour' in South Africa.

The result is, a method had to be devised for punishing the "Ganger lot", for being virtually NCOs military law does not allow one to imprison them, short of a Court Martial. So Interpreters, Gangers and Dressers are practically divided into three Classes each i.e. I, II, III, and for punishment they are reduced in their classes which of course means a great reduction of pay, and are even reduced to Coolies again in extreme cases.

The Chinese are very highly paid – more than a Tommy, and more than they would ever get in their own Country….They are equally well fed … Their 'tea' is pure wish wash!

With regard to the Chinese language, and the difficulty of learning it, one has one great consolation and that is that the ordinary Chinese Labourer doesn't understand it or speak it himself! It is said, if you know about 40 words, you know more than enough. In China there are so many dialects, and each community only knows its own, that only a limited number of words are interchangeable. These few words the labourers jabber away to themselves, gesticulating a great deal, and laughing. In fact they are a cheery crew. As they march to work they are always smoking, laughing and whistling, and one in twenty salutes because it amuses him to do so. You are not allowed to teach him to do so, but as the Chinese are born mimics, some of them will copy the NCO's. Their neatness is wonderful, they pat down a path or a grave or the side of a road until it is like a billiard table. I have seen a squad of them brushing the village street outside my billet and the Ganger going for a labourer because he had overlooked a hairpin on the road. Such a state of "neatness" as Noyelles was kept in, must be quite unknown in its history.

At the moment they are allowed to dress as they like and wear in fact the quilted garments that they came from China in, but I believe next year they are to have khaki. They have a great fancy for weird head dress, principally a sort of parsonic hat. One labourer in my company managed to secure a Lingari ribbon and was the envy of all. Their loose blue breeches always amuse me, about 8 inches too long in the seat. This gives them comfortable room to squat (as they habitually rest) with their 'tails' 3 inches from the ground.

A lot of rubbish has been written about the honesty, cleanliness etc of the Chinese. Take them all in all they are no cleaner or honester than anyone else. It's true that if they get boiling water they love washing, but cold water they won't go near. The great secret is to treat them absolutely honestly. Thus if they have been promised a holiday, they must jolly well have it, whether unforeseen events occur, which make it difficult, almost impossible for them to have it. If you thwart them they are likely to mutiny and then they get quite beyond control.

While at Noyelles they had a whole holiday to celebrate their 'harvest home'. A long programme had been drawn up of sports but it was rather hard to make them stick to it. They went off at tangents, building themselves up like a pack of cards and then all tumbling down, much to their amusement (not to mention mine) instead of sticking to the programme.

Graves of deceased Chinese labourers. (LEST supplementary 39a)

Then when the Tug of War came on, they pulled for a bit on either side, but if one side looked like being beaten, half a dozen of the "audience" hung on to the rope notwithstanding the expostulations of the referee. The Lady Mayoress attended and as I was the only officer who could talk French I had to do the honours!

The terms of service on which the Chinese are engaged, is for manual work behind the Line, and it remains to be seen whether they will 'stick it' if they are placed too far forward (as they are) where they are bombed or shelled.

Several companies are engaged at Dunkirk which place is continually under fire. More than once they have broken out of their compound there and bolted off in all directions. Some got half way to Paris and it took days getting them all together again.

Also the question of warmth will also crop up. All these Chinese are drawn from Northern China with a view to their hardihood. They first came over in, I think, April this year, but in the hottest of weather in early September they were marching off to their work with thick great coats on and the collars turned up; I have my doubts as to they will get through the winter in Northern France. But these are only mine own inferences.

It is not generally known the large numbers of Chinese we have working in France. In the spring of this year [1917] some 40,000 came over. By the time I was in Noyelles we had well over 100 Companies of say 500 each, i.e. 50,000. 40,000 more were due to arrive when I left Noyelles, and by March next year [1918] there will be 150,000 to 200,000 employed in France: at road making, tree felling, dock work, railway work, with the tanks, and labour of all descriptions.

[LeStrange was posted to a company in Calais on 24 October.]

CALAIS

We arrived at Calais in pouring rain and pitch dark, and with no porters available took half an hour collecting kit. By this time it was past black out…. I walked across the station yard and took up our quarters at the Hotel Metropole. A very 4th rate concern but I was thankful to have a roof over my head. I made friends with a Canadian (Captain Hughes) who was very home-sick! With whom I dined, and afterwards Woodgate came in and we sat up until 11 o'clock having a cheery talk in the 'bar'. The next morning at 8 o'clock I started off to walk across the town and docks, to find No. 6 Rest Camp, close to which Col Towne, OC 2nd Labour Group hung out. As I anticipated he is a charming man. I begged him to let me stay in a billet but he said it was really against all regulations, and that I must be with my Company. A blizzard was blowing at this time (it was very hard to stand up) and the sandstorm was blinding, but I started off to find a vacant tent. Eventually I got a thing like a bathing hut, but with the sides of brown paper and of course yellow paper in the windows which takes the place of glass in these regions. There was an inch of sand on the floor and it was quite bare. I again got boxes and planks and blankets and did what was possible to make it habitable, then went back to the town and fetched, not my kit, but my haversack with a toothbrush etc – but enough of this 'grousing'. I can only say life was a misery and it was impossible to keep warm.

I was told my Company, no.70, had mutinied the week before owing to bad handling, that they were a very rough lot, and required careful management. A nice start! However I had 2 capital subs in Lts Saunders and Smith (the other two, Randall and Rodgers, being away on leave!) and they were of the greatest help to me. Our working hours at the docks were from 3 am to 10 pm but of course my subs did most of the night work, and I only went down to the work (a mile off) occasionally. Most of my time was taken up in my Orderly Room where I had a capital Sergeant Major.

This went on for about a week, when I was daily getting more rheumatic and had a devil of a cold, so I went to Towne and told him it was either a question of a billet in the town, or hospital. He said, I think you had better carry out both your ideas for I can see you are quite unfitted to stand this climate. So back I went to the Metropole and also applied for a [Medical] Board …

The raids have been frequent, though seldom is any mention made of them in the papers. There are 4 strong 'hooters' placed round the town and these blessed things make the most weird and ghastly noise every 15 minutes from the time of the first alarm until it is over. The 'hooter' goes by the name of 'Mournful Mary', and being within 150 yards of one as I was, the row was quite as bad as the bomb dropping. The Boshes are determined to 'get' the locks and docks, but up to the present have failed. One night when in the Hotel, 2 bombs were dropped, one on either side of it, about 200 yards off. Roughly they raid Boulogne weekly, Calais 4 nights out of 7, and Dunkirk, in which there is no civil population and is quite flattened out, almost daily.

On one occasion at dinner I met a Captain Woodhouse and the conversation turned on the 'Kitchener Rumour'. He said that he had positive proof that K of K was alive and imprisoned in Heligoland. He was prepared to offer 'any odds' on it. So with due formality he made me the bet of £100 to £10 on it, to be paid within a month of the finish of the war. (Good business!)

[Lestrange went into Hospital on 2 November.]

HOSPITALS

I have been in 4 Military Hospitals – the best and the worst – and I never want if possible to find myself in another! King Edward VIII's hospitals leave nothing to be desired; Lady Mary Meynell's is run on much slacker lines and there are VADs (forgetful and flighty) and No. 30 General at Calais has no comforts of any sort, you are in a hut with 6 others, no heating, bad food, badly lit, the EC and washing hut 70 yards off (to which all 'walking cases' have to go), rotten doctors and orderlies, in fact no-one or nothing pleasant, except kind and willing nursing staff. But, good or bad, to my mind all these hospitals have the same horrible drawback. Sleep is an impossibility. First there is the 'owner of the house' then the matron, a doctor, a surgeon, an orderly, a waiter, several nurses, some VAD helpers, some dozen people, who are in and out of a ward at least every ¼ hour day and night. It's enough to drive one mad and is made worse when there are cases in the ward which require constant dressing.

RETURN TO ENGLAND

On Nov 7th just over 2 months since I landed in France I left Calais on my return far more dramatic than when I started and having failed to be of the slightest use to my country – or any prospect of being!

We (6 of us) left the Hospital at 7 am, on an ambulance for the Garde Maritimes. There was bright sunshine, and after having got aboard a full complement of 'cases', we set forth at 9.30. Having got ½ a mile outside the Harbour we "pulled up" to await our escort of destroyers. There was a heavy sea running and the Chief Medical Officer told me their last evening's crossing had been the worst of the year. Then we knocked about for an hour and a half before we made a fresh start. Outside Calais on the southern beach, a 'ZZ boat' had run aground, and there also, remained portions of an aeroplane which we had brought down. It contained what was left of the pilot, the observer, and another Hun, clothed in French uniform, who was evidently being landed as a spy. After a very 'rolly' passage we got to Dover at 12.15 and then more waiting began. Till 4.15 we were kept there, for the Boulogne hospital ship to come in and unload her cargo into our train. At last we started – at a very slow pace for London and eventually pulled up at Charing Cross about 7 o'clock – just 12 hours journey! By luck I was posted to Lady Mary Meynell's hospital, 8 Lennox Gardens, and I was thoroughly thankful to turn in, in comfort and warmth, after a good dinner.

25.11.17.

11

GALLIPOLLI

Norfolk men fought across the world: there were many in Gallipoli for example. The Norfolk Record Office has a full diary by Geoffrey Barker describing his time there:

Thursday 23 September:
Sent things home by Rush. Left Leiston 6.40, arrived Liverpool 4.30. John Woodhouse produced a good lunch. Marsala on train. Helped to serve out drinks to troops at bar at Peterboro' sta. Crowds cheered train thro' Cheshire. Men had chalked train with notices re Turkish Delight all over. Marched onto Olympic. Enormous ship. Got good cabin with fan on 'C' deck with Pemberton. The Palm Court turned into armoury, most of the ship transformed. Officers dine in 2nd class saloon and use 1st class Smoking Room and Top Deck. Sergeants have the Restaurant. Our Reg't is in the 3rd class saloon in hammocks. O.C. ship Brig Gen Hoare.

Friday 24 September:
Authorities v worried because everyone's friends know the name of the ship and 150 telegrams have arrived addressed to the ship and reports of submarines are many and varied. Men's messing arrangements in awful muddle. Ship never been used as transport before and no one knows where to find anybody else. We stop in the Mersey all day but no one allowed on shore.

Saturday 25 September:
Sail about 10.15 am escorted by 3 Torpedo Boats. Go straight into Irish Channel, course for a time NW, so we think may be taken round N of Ireland, but we then turn south. Pass Holyhead going all out at tea time. In afternoon alarm goes. I go to watertight doors of Reg't and have them shut thus securely locking in most of W Somerset Yeo. 'Orders is orders' but it seems mad. Eventually allowed to let them out.

Sunday 26 September:
Church Parade for 4 men per troop! We have a new chaplain named Blencoe, seems a good sort, has done a good deal of work in Solomon Is. 4 in[ch] gun on poop fires a couple of shells, everyone jumps and thinks it's a submarine. Destroyers have left us. All day out of sight of land, strong wind and heavy sea. A good many men sick but feel fit myself. There is a gymnasium on board so get to exercise them. H saw the Norfolks singing 'Oh bring back my charger to me'.

Monday 27 September:
Parade at 9.30 as usual – v tedious. No room to do anything but a little physical drill. Our maxims are mounted on the decks and practice a little at nothing in particular. Hear of big advance in France. We go v slow, sea calm but getting hot. Find swimming baths and have a swim, but it's v hot there too. Play Bridge with Redmond, Hugh and John Woodham, lose 3 rubbers.

Tuesday 28 September:
Course now E all day, so we must have gone a long way into Atlantic and are now going for Gibraltar. Told we shall not stop anywhere before our port of destination, we suppose this is Mudros. Hoare tells off all the officers in the Smoking Room for portholes being open, troop decks not clean enough. News comes that Keir Hardie is dead, all the troops cheer! Yarn goes round that Turkish snipers get paid 1/- for each private they get, 10/- for each officer, 20/- for each officer of field rank or over, and get fined £2 for each staff officer they get! So tell Hugh. Pass Gib about 9 pm, Ceuta and Algeciras lighted up. We steam v slowly no lights.

Wednesday 29 September:
All day going fairly fast about 2–5 miles from African coast. Pass Algiers at 4 pm, seems a big town.

Thursday 30 September:
Still due east, pass one or two small islands, still hug African shore which is now flatter. Leave Malta to north at night but don't see it.

Friday 1 October:
Draw men's helmets out of store and pay wine bills, with biggest 6/- bottle for Mumm this is not much. In afternoon pick up two boatloads of French sailors (about 35 of them) who had been put in boats and their ship (a cargo boat) sunk by enemy submarine at 9 am. Seemed quaint to meet them in open boats on a calm sea and out of sight of land. At 4 am alarm, submarine periscope seen 1½ miles off, some say closer. All troops on deck in lifebelts, we turn right round and steam W, then zigging about a lot, then W. We have not steered N by SW but are getting near the end of the trip.

Saturday 2 October:
Arrived at Lemnos, magnificent harbour protected by double line of torpedo nets, two villages E and W Mudros on each side, 9 miles apart by land. Any amount of British and French

battleships, cruisers and craft of all kinds, but nearly all old. About one or two hospital ships brilliantly lighted at night. Hear we are to stop on board for the present.

Sunday 3 October:
Go on shore with Pemberton after great difficulty in getting leave and a boat. See E Mudros a small Greek village, inhabitants talk Greek, soil a sort of yellow brittle dusty clay. V little vegetation, only see about ½ doz trees (wretched looking figs and olives, no fruit). Camps and wooden buildings up and under construction everywhere, and jetty being built and roads made, chiefly by French Algerian troops. We buy matches as these are getting scarce on board. The Camps are nearly all French but the 10th Div'n (English) are there too, and we see officers who tell us their Div'n has been on Gallipoli for a week and come back, only about ½ their men still fit and are refitting they think for a new expedition (? Shall we be told to join them). We pass a seaplane depot ship and various submarines. See French sick lines for horses and mules and a motor but nothing of great interest. There are masses of stores on shore and mountains of timber, hay and straw. When we get back we find the men have been knocked off milk with their tea as it has been requisitioned for the hospitals. They might do the same with the fizz we get so cheap for dinner! See Greek square-rigged schooners carrying timber come in, v pretty. Hear Bulgaria is likely to come in against us! Flies v bad on shore.

Monday 4 October:
Parade as usual in the morning. It is now not so very hot as it was a few days ago. Send letter by hand to Ingy uncensored. I wonder how he's getting on. I hope he'll get it.

Tuesday 5 October:
We coal, a filthy proceeding but as our top deck is 64 ft above the waterline it's above the worst of it. In the evening Duncannon leaves suddenly for a staff job at Imbros, without saying goodbye to a soul, not even the F.G. who got him into the Reg't. Directly he heard we were for the trenches he went to London to get this job! And when on the ship got himself promoted Capt to put himself in a better position to take the job. The Col and Walter are the only two who knew of his little game and ought to be ashamed of themselves.

Wednesday 6 October:
Still coaling. Alarm about midday to get ready to leave tonight. Soon cancelled, we are to stop on boat till Friday. In afternoon am told that Walter, G, Cadogan, self, Leslie and Ginn are to be left reserve. I get Pym to see Bgde Major to try and alter it, but it's no good. Awfully sickening not to be allowed to take my troops when they first go into action. Later hear there has been a Board on the Lord Nelson which officially decided that we had a torpedo fired at us on Oct 1st from about 1,000 yds.

Thursday 6 October:
Jack Crossley turns up at lunch, seems to have a pretty soft job on the *Amazon* (Headquarters ship).

Friday 8 October:
The Reg't left in the afternoon, left with Walter, Guinness, Cadogan, Leslie and Ginn. 38 men as detail. Most awful afternoon seeing them off. Couldn't say goodbye to any of them. V bad night.

Training in Norfolk at North Walsham camp. (MC 2283/1)

Training in Norfolk at Cromer. (MC 2283/1)

Saturday 9 October:
Ordered to leave with details at 2. Awful muddle, we finally got into small boat at 5 and land in darkness at 6.30. Decide to leave heavy baggage on boat, bivouac where we land. No water, have ½ bottle fizz stolen from my valise, I suppose guard was thirsty? About midnight woken up, all baggage to be off the boat, awful job getting it all off and stacking the cases in the dark.

Sunday 10 October:
Go to our camp with the baggage in motor lorry, about 4 miles off, find others there. V pretty spot, but all water has to be carried ½ mile and must be boiled. All tents had to be put up again in new places, and endless fatigues to be done. Walter shared tent with Redmond B, the rest of us in one tent. Good view over bay SW of Island.

Afternoon went with Leslie to bay and had splendid bathe. Took boat to SS Osiris lying off, and got provisions from Canteen on board, dried figs etc. Tea on beach off mixed biscuits and figs. First English girl I'd seen since England came riding by.

Monday 11 October:
Biked down to Turks' head pier, roads awful. Went by ferry to Store Ship Minnetorka, bought cutlery, plates etc for Mess. Met v good fellow – de la Tour. Had v bad gin and bitters with him.

Tuesday 12 October:
Walked in afternoon to Kontia, a v pretty Gk village about 2 miles off in valley (cultivated) Saw ch (rather like RC), and school, all the women were spinning cotton in the streets from little distaffs, and one was weaving. Bought condensed milk for Farrow who was sick, a touch of the sun I think. Several quite well built houses with small gardens, v eastern, and quaint windmills with 12 canvas sails. Got back at dusk and found orders to rejoin Reg'ts at 8 am next morning, best news for a long time, but had so much of orders cancelled that we refused to pack at all.

Wednesday 13 October:
Up at 6.30, breakfast 7, packed (Farrow ill so had to manage without him, can't do it as well as he does). Off at 9, march to pier, onto horrid little boat 'Sir Joseph Pease' & from that to a K M L boat 'El Kahira' which is taking us, stores, an Indian draft to Anzac, blowing hard but she's a steady boat. Heard a good deal of firing above as we landed. It was pitch dark when we reached the cove. I carried a crate of dixies into lighter where we all (W.H. Nk Yeo & selves) huddled together in a sort of black hole of Calcutta below decks for what seemed hours. No room for most men to sit even on the floor it was so close. Reached pier at last & got all baggage off. Got a man to take the dixies & he smashed the crate, only loss two lids. Dumped heavy luggage found Golder of Brigade Signal Troop as guide & started off with men carrying packs and kit bags. Left guard on heavy stuff as Australians took everything. A case of whisky was left by Nk Yeo with a man sitting on it to guard it, he was knocked off and case taken! Had two bottles brandy in my valise, but nothing so obvious as a wooden case! We turn from Wallie's Pier W through a sap, at first fork of which Golder leads us wrong. We go up the other one then after another ¼ hour Golder admits he's lost himself. He goes on to prospect but doesn't return in ½ an hour & has apparently lost us, so we go back to road by pier & lie down on road to wait from 1.45 am till dawn. I found a cosy nook out of wind, believe I was the only one of the party to get a good sleep! At 5.30 am telephone to Div Hqrs for another guide & get up to New

Bedford Road (a little valley in the hills) at 8, make tea and breakfast of cold bully and biscuits. Find chaplain and QMC and a few men from the Reg't the rest of the Reg't having just gone up to the fire trenches. Ingy rode up in the afternoon. Spend the rest of the day in arranging for Squadron Details and digging dug-out.

Friday 15 October: Valises etc didn't come up from beach so given another day before we rejoin Reg't, walk down to see Ingy with Apple in the afternoon.

Saturday 16 October:
At 11.30 take details to the Squadron who are in firing line under instruction from 11th London. Go thro' our section of trench, which runs v. like the Roman wall on the crest of a hill from a barricade across the Aghill Devry to Sandbag Ridge, the right hand section guarding the barricade. V. hilly, rising 15 ft in as many yards, trench too shallow and places for posts not yet properly dug. At left hand end near Sandbag Ridge we are opposite to the Turk over a saddle, towards which both sides are digging. We are at present about 250 yds apart. At the Barricade end we are 600 yards from the Turk, with a great valley filled with ravines and spurs between. We are issued with maps, good, about 1000 yards to 1", but as there are few spots we can definitely place, hard to read ... It seems v. heavy work, all the country covered with thick low scrub through which it is in some places impossible to go, & in all impossible to move quickly, except on the bottoms of the devrys where one can on a moonlight night be seen v. clearly.

Sunday 17 October:
Am rushed at every turn. Carry on in the trenches, when not there, working at my dug-out. Turks have a Moslem feast beginning today and we expect they may make an attack but they don't. John Woodhouse on night patrol. Am beach officer 9 -2, raining hard, so v difficult to get about in the mud.

Monday 18 October:
In the trenches, nothing particular doing till the evening when I went out along the Agkyll Devry under instruction in night patrol work. Moon bright. It seemed v nervy sort of work, as we had to go along the bottom of the white devry, as one made such a noise going through the bushes. We met no Turks however, but came across the body of a dead Gurkha and of a horse, both v far gone and v noisome.

Tuesday 19 October:
1/5 Beds take over trenches from 9th Londons. We are still under instruction from Beds, a v tough and efficient lot, under an extremely capable and energetic Col Brighton. One of their officers named Smyth was a clerk in our Cambridgeshire branch, and has established quite a reputation for himself as a scout on night patrol work. He had been out about 6 months and once had with a small party turned the Turks out of a listening post in a shallow trench on a spur running out towards our lines, a very fine feat, but the strain of this sort of work had obviously told on his nerves and he hoped he wd not have to be sent again.

While at the barricade in our lines across the Aghyl Devry a shrapnel shell fell within 6 yds of me but luckily didn't explode.

Training in Norfolk at Cromer. (MC 2283/1)

At 12.15 at night sent out with Tait, on night patrol under instruction, took Blowers, W R, with me. Tait took a Sgt and a Cpl. We first went and after some trouble found a Turkish listening post in a shallow trench about 3 ft deep on the end of a spur jutting out from the Aari Bair ridge to our lines. I was under instruction, so Tait went up first to reconnoitre… Luckily it was not held that night. Then we went down on the far side of a spur to a gulley at the head of which we had been told the Turks were working. The sides of the valley were covered with v thick scrub, we could barely get down. I made a tremendous row, or so it seemed. The bottom of the gulley was a white dry watercourse, up which we had to go, in a bright moon. After we had crawled up about 200 yds we were brought up short by a man's cough about 30 yds ahead of us. We lay still and waited 20 mins. He coughed from time to time but did not move, so we decided he must be part of a covering party over the workers we could hear talking and what sounded like putting up wire behind. We then crossed the devry and crawled to the next bend, about 10 yds further on and waited ¾ hr. It was now about 3.45 am and the moon was hidden by a hill, so we had the advantage of less light. We heard men talking and thought we heard movements on the hills on each side of us.

Then as we could learn no more by further waiting we decided that we must go on to find the force and disposition of their covering party by drawing fire. I took one side of the gulley followed by Blowers, Tait and his two men the other. We crept on. When we had gone 5 yds the sentry opened fire at about 15 yds at Tait, about 4 other Turks in the devry fired at the same time. We replied, I was too excited, fired high. About ½ doz men on the hill on our left and the same on the spur to our right rear fired too, but it was only at our flashes and no one was hit. They had obviously been trying to encircle us, but had not had quite time. As they were nearly round us we had to retire which we did pretty quick. 3 of the 5 of us tripped over stones and fell over and the Turks came on about 5 yds and I thought they wd try to rush us, but luckily were afraid and stopped. I reloaded to give the men time to get up with 2 cartridges, one of which misfired. The other went off, after which I stood helplessly clicking, then went after the others. We got off 17 rounds altogether, of which I fired 7, and so back to the trenches about ¼ mile away through the barricade. After the excitement they seemed quite like home! Back at 4.15, lay down for a bit, and up at 5 to report to Brighton.

Wednesday 20 October:
Last day under instruction from the Beds, was trench officer 2-6 am, 4th night running of night work – lucky that I can sleep at odd times! A shrapnel shell fell within 6 yds of me (in New Bedford Road) but luckily did not burst.

Thursday 21 October:
Relieved at 6.30 am to go back to rest camp and am given rather better dugout which I work at to improve. Tea with Ingy.

Friday 21 October:
Rest. Work at dugout etc.

Saturday 23 October:
The same.

Sunday 24 October:
Church Parade at 7. Take Pym down to Anzac to lunch with Ingy, and we stop to tea. Billy
Vincent there too. Ingy v fit and cheerful.

Monday 25 October:
Sent to go round the Australian trenches with Flint. V interesting, their trenches are deeper
and more neatly dug than ours. Saw a trench mortar that will send a 2 lb bomb up to 60 yds
with a rifle cartridge! Part of their trenches with enormously heavy timber and sandbag cover
were Turkish, which they captured. Trenches only 75 yds apart in places, so frequent bombing
stations etc and no firing except thro' loopholes. I saw Gaba Tepa, a fortified Turkish hill running
into the sea, from which they cd enfilade our trenches, but they have been so shelled there
they daren't use it except as an observation post. Their cookery seems better than ours, and
they are a far tougher lot. When I got back was told off to go to Anzac at 5 next morning with a
Brigade Fatigue Party to fetch officers' base kits from Mudros. Any amount of commissions for
all sorts of things given me from the Regt.

Oct 26, Tuesday: Left Anzac Pier at 6 am for Mudros with Stannard from my troop, a Norfolk
Yeoman and the R Q M S of Welch Horse. Went by HMS Partridge, a Clyde to Belfast boat.
After good breakfast had a hot bath, simply topping, the first since the Olympic. Reported on
the Amazon at midday and got a good lunch there, the staff seem to do themselves pretty
well. Landed at W Mudros at 3 and had good 4 mile walk to Yeomanry Details Camp. On the
way made friends with a Capt Creighton who was running a RAMC canteen, bought milk and
fruit to take back. Found Fraser of the Welch H[orse] in charge of Brigade stores and Capt
Marsham of E Kent Yeo in charge of camp. Shared Marsham's tent.

Resting outside Gunton Park during training in Norfolk. (MC 2283/1)

Shaving duties during training at North Walsham. (MC 2283/1)

Wednesday 27 October:
Went to OC Reinforcements in morning. Saw his staff captain, a nice fellow but an awful fool. He told me that having got to Lemnos I should find it hard to get off again! O C Col Fortescue out so went with my party to E Mudros and bought as much as I had money for at French Canteen and got it back, by great luck getting a motor lorry to take it up to the camp for me. At the camp were 29 officers' reinforcements from Paten's Yeomanry Divn. Two nights before they had been pitchforked onto our poor 3 officers with our divisional base kits at 7 pm, with only one servant between the 29 and all wanting dinner. Most marvellous of all, though entirely unexpected, they were provided for. They chiefly came from 2nd and 3rd line units, but were a v nice lot.

Thursday 28 October:
Spent morning repacking stores in cases for travelling. Afternoon got £5 more from Amazon and bought things I hadn't been able to get at exorbitant prices after much haggling in a Greek village with a pretty well-house at entrance. Any amount of Mil Police in village.
    Saw Col Fortescue, got orders to go back at 6 next morning. Woken up at 11 pm by order to say that boat to Anzac couldn't run next day owing to gale then blowing.

Friday 29 October:
Saw Marsham off early with Brigade Details to Helles and Suvla. Went onto Amazon and drew another £5 (why can't they let us get more at one time as it takes a good 3 hours to get it!! Red tape again). On to E Mudros, more stores and back again, finally packed up.

Friday 30 October:
Down at R E Pier with all stuff by 8.30 as ordered, no one seemed to expect us, and as a lighter had sunk off the end of it, it could not be used. Went and sent all over the shop for the M L O. At 11.0 he appeared saying he had kept a boat waiting for us since 9 at the South Pier over a mile away, would we embark at once. We had about 3 tons of stuff in all, Motor Transport said they could not move it, so he said we must wait another day! Fraser however bribed two transport drivers and we got off at 12. Again transhipped from the lighter to the El Kahira which made fast to the Amazon, drew another fiver to square debts. Left Mudros at 4 with a lot of Ghurka and Sikh drafts on board and arrived Anzac Cove about 10. Drafts had to be got off first and took till 1 in disembarking, in course of which 2 Ghurkas got slightly wounded in arm and leg by spent bullets.

Sunday 31 October:
Finally we got into lighter with … all our stuff about 4 am. Kept on taking cargo until 7.40 when a shell (shrapnel) came just over our heads, so we cast off to let the El Kahira get out of range. In another minute another came before we were clear and cut her stays between the masts, quickly followed by a third which covered her deck with bullets, but luckily no one hurt. We then steamed hard for the pier, and she went off quick too, dragging her anchor! Landed our stuff on the beach, put guard on it till it could be brought up at night, and went to Ingy for some breakfast. Up to the rest camp to which the Regt had returned that morning and reported at 11.0. Found all well, they had 5 days in the trenches without a single casualty, but dysentery had played the dickens with them, about 150 out of 450 in hospital, but all the officers fairly well. Church Parade in the evening.

Monday, 1 November:
Stores had come up, tremendously welcomed by all. Divided them out. Afterwards took Jamy to tea with Ingy and then he dined in our Squadron Mess. Felt awfully tired.

Tuesday 2 November:
Felt absolutely useless and weak, so lay down most of the day, luckily nothing I had to do, first time I've felt rotten since I landed.

Wednesday 3 November:
Put in a hard day's work at dugout as I felt better, but had to clear off to bed almost before the end of dinner.

Thursday 4 November:
Rained part of the day. Afternoon went round the part of the trenches I shall have to take over tomorrow.

Friday, 5 November:
Up to King's Own avenue, took over Posts 6-10 in Brighton's walk. T.O. 12–2 pm, 6–8, 12–2 am, v quiet day. Regt getting v low in numbers owing to dysentery, only 7 fit men for trench work in my troop and 49 in Sqn. McKeline ill. Frank Goldsmith and Nusker went to hospital this morning. Am looking after Lowestoft Troop for McKeline.

Saturday 6 November:
The weather is still lovely, but getting cold at nights, but as in the trenches one may not for the 5 days take off one's boots at night, it is not hard to keep warm. What one's blankets will be like after a muddy week is better left to the imagination. Poor old McKeline got worse this morning, had to be carried to hospital with 16 more from the Regt. T.O. 10–12 am, 8–10 pm and 12–2 am.

Sunday 7 November:
T.O. 8–10 am, 10–12 pm and 4–6 am. The boredom of this is perfectly awful when, as always seems the case, there is nothing doing. Mail and tobacco in.

Monday 8 November:
T.O. 6–8 am, 6-8 pm and 12–2 am. We get rumour that K of K has given up War Office and is coming out here.

Tuesday 9 November:
Same old sort of routine. Went out at midnight with Sgt Emeny on patrol, to locate sniper suppose[d] to shoot at our posts from foot of 'Bulgar Bluff'. Confirmed his existence and found where he was shooting from, which was what we wanted to do, but as he was in carefully chosen position and we should have had to give ourselves away by moving, did not try to get him.

A local offers some advice to men training in Norfolk. (MC 2283/1)

Trench warfare recreated in Norfolk. (MC 2283/1)

Wednesday 10 November:
Relieved at 6 am and back to New Bedford Lane, found my dugout had been improved somewhat by Firth who had it in my absence reroofed it, and put in a window. No water for washing to be got!

Brown arrived back from Imbros with £500 worth of provisions for the Bgde including a cockerel and 5 hens! What a familiar row he kicks up in the morning, the hens make no attempt to lay any eggs tho! Our Sq Mess share comes to about £16 worth, so we're in clover for a bit. Poor Apples went to hospital.

Thursday 11 November:
Deepen dugout. Take the Licett down to tea with Ingy at Anzac, the Turk has put 64 HE 82 shells into the next gully, smashing up the Div wireless store and doing a lot of damage. Ingy's Adjt comes out to tea, his dugout has been blown to blazes. We were nearly got by a shell as we past the Gully. The Turk seems to have now got more and better ammn.

Friday 12 November:
Still working at dugout. Brown has finished dividing up his stores and was disgracefully kicked by the Col – who was most offensive. Inoculated against cholera – no immediate effect.

Saturday 13 November:
In a court martial in the morning on a case of alleged self-maiming, obviously unintentional so man was let off.

Sunday 14 November:
Went to an early celebration, about 30 of all ranks there, v impressive, in the open with sounds of firing all round and a v rude table made of broken ration boxes.

Saw most interesting information from a deserter, Turks at night have adv posts lying out in front of their wire, relieved at midnight, these are what our patrols run into. The sniper who makes such good practice at the posts at the left end of our line appears to be a sniper who has a great reputation as a shot. Lunch with Ingy and Billy Vincent at Anzac, have to go round by Divn HQ as part of the Aghyl Deve is so much shelled that it's closed by day. On way back, went up to the trenches to look at posts we are to take over tomorrow, back for service in evening, but as the wind was wrong anyone who opened their mouth had it filled at once with smoke from the incinerator. For dinner some cheese and good bottled beer, how we do live!

Monday 15 November:
Took over trench lines at 6 am, v little been done since we left and no casualties. John Woodhouse rather bad with dysentery but carries on except for night work. By directing fire from two posts onto spot where I heard sniper on patrol last night of last turn, stopped sniping at two of our posts further up. T.O. 2-4, 8-10 pm and 2-4 am. Deepened dugout. Tremendous row of bombardment and blowing up of mines at Hill 60 at 5 o'clock but afterwards heard we did not gain much. As usual on our left Australians attacked Hackney Wick but had no luck. Last night Turks attacked our listening post but were driven off after wounding 4 of the 7 men in it, it was not held by our Regt. Storm at night, bed wet!

Tuesday 16 November:
First parcels arrived, watch, chocolate and Fortnum and Mason watch, most awfully welcome, specially choc which helped the night watches thro' in middle of afternoon. Day (Walter G's chauffeur) was killed by shrapnel case fired at one of our aeroplanes, it broke his neck…

Satuday 3 December:
Went back to rest camp, out of which we hear we are to [be] turned by N.Z.'s taking up our old line of trench. Desperate business being moved like this in December, no proper arrangements being made owing to Command's inability to think. Walked down to Anzac in afternoon and was missed by a shell by 20 yds in the open, passed 12 mules killed by another just before I got there. Found Ingy had left the night before, shall miss him v much, being able to drop in on v pleasant company and a good meal. Found the canteen stores from Imbros on the beach and got some oranges off them. The men with them had not been able to form a proper guard and a good deal of stuff had been stolen.

Sunday 4 December:
Rest Camp rather heavily shelled in morning, 1 killed and 3 wounded, all in gun section. Shell case came into Crisp and John's dugout but luckily John who was inside wasn't hurt. My bath and a pair of boots on roof of my dugout both cut up by bullets, one of which came thro' the tin. My troop is now reduced to 8 in all and Lowestoft to 9. Service and H.C. by ffolkes.

Monday 6 December:
A mail at last, letters from home but no parcels. The first for a fortnight. Also bread and meat which we have not had for 10 days, how one does enjoy them when they are scarce.

Tuesday 7 December:
Another mail. Letter from Miles who seems to have been having an exciting time.
 Regt now so much diminished by sickness that the Sq system is abandoned and Regt divided into 2 wings under Frank and Pym. Royce being 2nd in command. 1 wing with 80 men always to be in the trenches, and 25 of the other in Reserve Gully in support. To start on Thursday as even with present numbers a wing can't produce 80 effectives. Division breaks down at once, and all round borrowing of men has to start. Makes it v complicated, Ord Rm don't even try to work it out, leaving it entirely to a series of supplementary questions by Sq Leaders to develop. Result, only Pym's ability prevents chaos and some men being in trenches more or less indefinitely.

Wednesday 8 December:
Regt is supposed to shift to rest Camp tomorrow, however there's nowhere ready to go to. However Pym by seeing N Z major who is to take over R C gets leave to stay where we are until they definitely want to come in.

Thursday 9 December:
Right wing up in trenches, I take 25 men to reserve Gully in support, but get leave to come back for meals. All day spent arranging fatigues which my 25 men have to do for the men in the trenches, and in getting tin etc and digging to get cover for them for the night.

Norwich tank week, held to raise funds for the war effort, April 1918. (ETN 6/12/14)

Norwich tank week, held to promote the sale of war bonds. (ETN 6/12/14)

Friday 10 December:
Still in support, at night it was reported that some Turks were on our parapet in a thinly held part of the line, but we weren't called out.

Saturday 11 December:
Back at Rest Camp.

Sunday 12 December:
Nothing doing but felt v rotten, it turned out to be jaundice coming on.

Monday 13 December:
Walked down to Anzac to get boots out of Ordnance, as one pair has worn out and another holed. Met an R. E. subaltern on the A.N.Z.A.C. staff who told me that Suvla's Anzacs were being evacuated, that ¾ of the heavy artillery had already been taken off, and any amount of stores etc. That if the weather was good they hoped to have everyone off by 11.30 pm Sat Dec 18th. This was absolutely the first news that any of our Regt of this. One thought of Lord Ribblesdale and felt what an awful indiscretion he had made, and also of estimates reported to have been made by the staff that an evac would cost us anything from 10% to 25% of the troops concerned. Went on to see Brown at Divn HQ had a talk with him and a most grateful bottle of beer! He was bound to secrecy but I gathered that what I had heard wasn't far from the truth. 12" shrapnel had been served out to the ships to cover the last retiring parties if the Turks should attack.

Back to lunch, felt absolutely rotten and tired out. Found an order to pack valises to weigh not more than 25 lbs, all other kit to be left at dump. My sleeping bag and other treasures all have to be scrapped. Go up to trenches while officers come down and pack their kit. While we are there Turks bombard our line with 6" H.E. just beyond our Right toward Hill 60. Any amount of bits of shells fly back over us, some even to the rest gully, but no one hurt in our section. Tuttle and 40 men go off as an advance party with our kits, we don't know where to.

Tuesday 14 December:
Up to the trenches at 6 am, take over Bile's dugout. Royce is O.C. trenches. Eddis the bombing officer told off to go with advance party, so Eversdon takes his place. Pryor, John and Crisp (sick) make up the officers of the wing, the men a v mixed lot of all the Sqns. Eversdon v keen on making all sorts of quaint bombs. V little wire in front of trenches, so we put out a lot more, preparing for our shift.

Wednesday 15 December:
Still feeling bad, so see Dr and find it's jaundice. I lie up most of the time in my dugout and mayn't eat most of the things we are finishing off so as to stop the Turks getting 'em. When in Rest Camp to see the Dr find fatigue party burying rifles and ammn, a reserve of 12,000 rounds buried as well as a lot of other odd stuff. All our kits burned and all men's kits except a little private stuff. They are only allowed to take 1 blanket, 1 waterproof cape, 1 pr of socks, and greatcoat and 2 days' rations. And last (C) Party not allowed to take blankets (entrenching tools all to be left).

Tommy sent off with 25 men in advance, leaving only about a dozen men in reserve. However, Turks seem v weak in front of us and have shown no sign of attacking, tho' our artillery fire has been practically confined to naval guns for the last week, and what sounds like one or two mountain guns constantly moved about and firing H.E. and shrapnel alternately. At night we try the effect of a cease fire, result that Turks practically cease firing too and show no signs of attacking.

Thursday 16 December:
Dr says I've got jaundice, am still feeling rotten and lie up all day. We put out more wire and get our orders for evacuation. Nearly all the remainder of the reserve under Crisp, who is getting better, to leave on Sunday evening, and on Monday the remainder in 3 parties, A, B and C. A leaving at dusk, B with the M[achine] Guns, Col and HQ at 8.30, and C at 12.30, with Tomkin, Pym and Eversdon, to go under Kensington straight down to beach at the nearest point, and acting as rear guard a temporary staging being put up and the party being taken off in naval cutters and then towed to trawlers which wd take them to Mudros.

Friday 17 December:
Still destroying kits and equipment at night. A tremendous blaze over Anzac where ordnance stores had been set light to, it looked as if it must be a certain warning of our departure to the Turk!

Soldiers in camp, perhaps in Gallipolli. (MC 2847/R3)

Practising trench digging on Felmingham Heath. (MC 2283/1)

Norfolk soldier Captain S. D. Page wrote from Gallipoli to a friend in Norwich – the letter was written on 17 September 1915, but did not reach Norwich until early November:

Our Regiment were fortunate enough to come out on the 'Aquitania' and her size enabled us all to very much enjoy the voyage. As we passed the points of interest on the way out it was most pleasing to note the eagerness and delight of the men whose previous outlook extended very little beyond their own country. We finally anchored in Lemnos Bay, and as we steamed in it certainly was a most wonderful sight. The Bay itself presents a most perfect harbour, and we were surrounded by literally hundreds of ships of all descriptions battleships of all nations, even including Japanese, submarines, torpedo destroyers, cruisers, transports – and as we steamed by our band playing the National Anthem and the 7,000 troops that we were carrying lining several deep every available inch of deck, all the larger ones 'dipped' in our honour. The thousands of troops, white men, black men, Indians, Egyptians, and apparently every nation save Germans, turning the whole scene into a hive of industry, and a picture which will for ever live in the minds of those of us who witnessed it. From here we were conveyed in small lighters to the peninsula, and landed at dusk at a new spot. Naturally we quickly found ourselves in the thick of the fighting, and it was most gratifying to see how splendidly our boys from the city factories conducted themselves, never flinching from everything. I must own that although I have lived in such close touch with them for the past twelve months and know and understand them thoroughly well, I was surprised and proud of them. For fourteen days we never had our boots or clothes off: we never washed so much as our hands, and hardly had any sleep. By day we were fighting or moving our positions, at night we were digging, always digging. Then we were relieved and sent back to the rest trenches. During this period we lived on bully beef, army biscuit, and a very little jam, and with the exception of three days, when we got some hot tea, we just had a pint of water per day. Water has been our great difficulty and our chief hardship. We simply could not get it, and with the frightful heat which we are not used to the men really had a grumble. This, of course, was an exception due to a new landing and was unavoid able; now however we have established ourselves and things are getting normal. The men are quite well fed, and even get rice and oatmeal served out to them, and water is now plentiful.

Another letter came from Private P. S. S. Munro, British Mediterranean Force, 26 December 1915:

We have been out here just months, yet it seems like two years, and one forgets what day of the week or month it is, every day seems alike. Out here we do a fortnight in the trenches and a fortnight at the rest camp, if one can call it such, for while at this so-called rest camp we have a daily fatigue of six hours digging. This is not my idea of a rest I can assure you.

I have had one or two very weird experiences in the trenches. A week or two back while our miners were sapping under the Turkish lines, they broke into the enemies' sap and three of us were told off with loaded rifles, revolvers and bombs to watch for the appearance of the Turks. Several times during the night we were bombed out, but we settled two or three of them, and in the end blew them, sap and all, into the air. You can imagine us sitting there during the night, we dare not have a light, we couldn't speak, but just listen and fire at the slightest noise.

I firmly believe the Turks don't wish to fight, but I suppose there are some Germans forcing them to do so. Turks very often give themselves up, and they have a very cunning method of doing so. If they leave their own trench without a rifle they are shot by their own men, and if they come into our trench with a rifle the same fate awaits them. So they leave their own trench with a rifle, drop it half way, and jump into our trench shouting 'Allah', 'Prisoner'.

The weather has changed with a vengeance now, from great heat to extreme cold, mixed with occasional torrential rain. On two occasions last week we were completely washed from our dug-outs, three inches of rain falling in less than three-quarters of an hour. We walked about, lit fires, made tea etc, and waited for dawn; when it did arrive we had to rescue rifles, rations, blankets and equipment absolutely covered with mud. If this is a sample of the rainy season which lasts two months I can see us being washed clean into the sea.

Just now we are living on bully beef, bread, and eternal apricot jam. No-one here has ever been known to have found an apricot in the jam, so we have to imagine they're in there. I think I'll leave jam severely alone after this war. Butter on our bread will be just grand when we do get it.

For many Norfolk people, the war was their first experience of the world beyond their home county. Some letters and diaries show an appreciation of new scenery and new ways of life, but, of course, there was a terrible price being paid: many thousands of Norfolk men lost their lives in Greece, Gallipoli and the Middle East.

12

ANIMALS AT WAR

The war involved the use of animals, especially horses, and many thousands were requisitioned from Norfolk farms to pull guns and carry ammunition on the Western Front. As Laura Stuart wrote in the *Carrow Works Magazine* (April 1915),

Many of us have wondered sadly what becomes of the horses commandeered by the Army. What, for example, is likely to be the fate of the pair of magnificent horses from Carrow Works which were claimed by the military authorities in the early days of the war – those horses which, being taken to the military camp nearby, seized a stray chance of escape and galloped back towards their old stable at Carrow works?

Her answer was that wounded horses were being cared for better than in any previous war. The Army Veterinary Corps had the duty of collecting wounded and abandoned horses. Those which were slightly wounded were given help at once; the seriously wounded ones were moved to 'horse hospitals'.

Laura Colman quoted from an account by Miss C. B. Duff of North Walsham, who had 'recently visited some of the Veterinary Hospitals in the North of France':

There are some thousand horses in the hospital, and they are divided into various wards according to their illness, the worst cases being in one part, and those suffering from pneumonia and colds in another, while the convalescents were further off in a part of the wood by themselves. They were nearly all of them doing extraordinarily well in spite of the incessant rain and of the mud in which they had to stand. The worst wounded horses were kept in some barns and sheds.

No horse is operated on without chloroform, and very often painful dressings are treated with local anaesthetics. I was specially interested to hear how the horses trust their nurses, and how, after the first time, they welcome the dressing of their wounds,

Animals played a vital role in many fields of war ... (MC 2847/R3)

... including bringing up the beer! (MC 2847/R3)

realising that the treatment will lessen the pain. The recoveries many of these horses make are most wonderful; I saw on very fine officers charger who had been shot right through his neck, and had to have several operations before his wound healed; he was absolutely fit, and there seemed no sensitiveness of any kind when the scar on his neck was touched. That the horses are not sad in hospital was amusingly illustrated to me when some eighty of them were brought from the convalescent side to a remount camp some four miles away. The moment they were let out in their new paddocks they galloped round, jumped the fences and hedges, and started back to their hospital as fast as they could possibly go.

Wounded horse after being chloroformed. (*Carrow Works Magazine*)

A dog used to carry a
communication system.
(*Carrow Works Magazine*)

Caring for horses in the trenches.
(*Carrow Works Magazine*)

13

THE END

The end came on 11 November 1918. The Armistice was declared as the guns fell silent after over four years of war. Bells rang out from Norfolk churches and there was general rejoicing. The school magazine records how the news of the Armistice was received at the Norwich High School:

On the morning of November 11th at 11.15 am the news that Germany had accepted our Armistice and that hostilities would therefore cease was brought by hand to the High School. In a very few minutes the glad news spread all over the School, and was received by Mistresses and girls alike with the greatest enthusiasm and excitement. Orders were received from Miss Wise [the headmistress] that we should all assemble in the Prayer Hall as quickly as possible. Very soon all the Forms were standing in their places. 'Now thank we all our God' was then sung with great vigour and joyfulness by all. Then Miss Wise gave out that all home-work should be excused and a holiday taken the following day. Canon Meyrick was present, who, after the hymn had been sung and the particulars of the Armistice had been read, spoke a few words bearing on the great day of the cessation of hostilities and of England's deliverance from her greatest enemy, at the same time announcing that there would be a great Thanksgiving Service at St Peter Mancroft Church in the evening, where everybody might have the opportunity of rendering thanks to God for the blessing of peace. The School then marched out in order through the Central Hall and front doors and lined up on the gravel square facing the School. The new, and very fine Union Jack was then hoisted into the bright and sunny morning from the Library window by Miss Salt, assisted by Miss Howard and Miss Carr, during which process 'God save the King' was sung, led by Miss Diver. This concluded, Phyllis Kent, the head girl, gave three cheers for all the Allies.

However, many were unable to share in the celebrations. Many were still feeling the loss of loved ones, such as Jessie Wainwright. Her son Samuel ('Chappie'), a lieutenant in the 6th Battalion, Norfolk Regiment, was killed in action on 12 March 1917; he was twenty-seven years old. She confided her pain to her diary:

Tuesday 12 March [1918]:
First anniversary of my darling Chappie's untimely and cruel fate, and oh the sadness of today for me, and the aching of my heart.

Tuesday 16 July:
A day of memories deeply sad for me:
   July 16th 1916: my darling Chappie wrote me he had signed his name for active service, which ended in the sacrifice of his most precious life.
   July 16th 1917: I sent a wreath to Achiel-le-Petit which eventually was put on his grave.
   July 16th 1918: The hated Huns possess Achiel-le-Petit and I am praying his grave may be kept safe, and I have put a long spray of rambler as I did last year, but have placed it on his bureau in the hall, being unable to get anything to him this year.

Thursday 22 August:
My wedding day, 30 years today – and my heart aches at the sorrow that has come to me, my Darling Chappie come and gone (in the flesh) but in the spirit ever here with me, dearest dearest son. His sacrifice is monstrous, cruel and wicked, and should never have been – but to think of him is ever the sweetest of my thoughts.

Thursday 15 October:
Two years ago this evening my Chappie darling went back to Flixton Camp, left his S. B. [Sam Browne] belt, sent it on to him there.

Sunday 10 November:
Day full of wild hopes 'Peace. In view. Germany utterly defeated, these hellish fiends will get their desserts.

Monday 11 November:
Peace – joy and love and glad hope for the future for some, for some sadness indescribable as for me, with the best gone out of my life, and the beautiful hope of years taken – and such a son, fine, manly, brave, tender and true, with loving kindness and dear thoughts for everyone and no thought for himself, such he was and such he will live in my heart and before my eyes, as long as life lasts God bless my boy.

Tuesday 12 November:
And everything is chaos bells ringing and thanks rending the air. I quiet myself by keeping on at my household work and ways and not paying any heed to it at all I could not bear to – my cup is full! of bitter sadness and I dare not think too much.

Most schools did not have any special celebrations on 11 November 1918. This may have been because it was an armistice, a suspension of hostilities, rather than the actual end of the war. It may also be because many Norfolk schools were suffering a new crisis which took their minds away from the war. This was the 1918 outbreak of influenza known as 'Spanish flu', which spread across the world and killed as many people as the war itself.

School logbooks are a good source for tracking its spread through Norfolk. It was very bad at St Philip's infant school, Norwich, in October. On 29 October, all the children well enough to come to school were paraded in the playground and told either to play outside or to go on an organised walk: 'This has been arranged in order to give the children the benefit of the open air if possible to prevent the spread of influenza.'

On 1 November, the headmistress at Kirby Bedon school found one of the teachers, Miss Nobbs, to be 'evidently in the first stages of influenza' and she was sent home. The school closed two days later. It reopened on 18 November, but only thirty-eight out of eighty pupils turned up. It was closed once more until 2 December, but this time just nine children came. The school was then closed for the rest of the term, reopening after the Christmas holidays in the first week of January.

The logbook at Baconsthorpe noted on 4 November that 'there is scarcely a home in the village where there is no-one ill'. The school was closed for three weeks. It reopened on 25 November but it was noted that 'very few scholars are from Hempstead where the epidemic has now spread'.

Just thirty-one out of the sixty children on the books turned up at Cranworth school on 13 November, and the school was closed until 8 December. The epidemic reached Stow Bedon later in the month, the school closing on 25 November. The closure was originally for a fortnight but was then extended until the end of term, so that the children in effect had a holiday period of over six weeks before the school reopened on 6 January 1919, as did the pupils of very many Norfolk schools – sadly, the majority of the children were probably too ill to enjoy the extended break.

For most sick children, it was a question of spending a few days in bed, but there were deaths when influenza became pneumonia. To take just one example, three young children died in Norwich on a single day: 5 November 1918. They were Dorothy Seaman (aged seven) of Suffolk Street, Alice Buttifant (aged five) of Ashby Street and Cyril Baker (aged two) of Walpole Street. In each case, the father was away in the armed forces, which must have meant great emotional stress for the mother; in these homes there can have been little celebration of the Armistice just six days later.

Adults were taken ill as well. Jessie Wainwight noted in her diary:

Thursday 14 November:
Influenza or something like it is rife everywhere – many are falling victims to this scourge – Have had to send the under girl to N and N Hospital today, very bad, think it best to clear the home of it.

Influenza affected soldiers as well, and there were fatalities among Norfolk's fighting men, such as Herbert Powell who died of influenza in France on 17 October 1918. Another victim was George Temple of the Royal Naval Air Service; his influenza developed into pneumonia and he died at Mudros aboard a hospital ship on 3 December 1918. He was twenty-one years old.

Commonwealth war grave at Caister;
note the man's age, sixty-five.
(Author's collection)

Cross of Sacrifice, erected where there
were twenty-five or more war graves
in a cemetery. (Author's collection)

Naturally, the disease struck those already weakened especially hard. Eight soldiers died of influenza at the Town Close Hospital in Norwich in November 1918, some of whom were probably already hospital cases. Not all were, however; three were men of the Pembrokeshire Yeomanry who had been in camp at North Elmham. Two of the victims were local men – Reginald King was a private in the Norwich Labour Battalion and Joseph Parrick, of Old Catton, was a corporal in the Royal Field Artillery.

Another influenza victim was Susannah Hall, a nurse from Reedham, who succumbed while serving in France in March 1919. Her name, not originally included, has since been added to the local war memorial.

14

AFTERMATH

The war had brought devastation everywhere. It had left many millions of widows and orphans, and many millions of starving people. Norfolk men and women were not slow to help. One was Beatrice Gurney, a Quaker in her late fifties. She joined the Church Army, like William Hewetson mentioned in an earlier chapter, and went to Namur in Belgium. Her task was to provide facilities for soldiers still stationed there, but she was so shocked by the things she saw that she took it upon herself to provide a party for some of the little orphans in the city.

29 July 1919:

Yesterday Miss Marriott and I went to see the sisters' orphanage and came home very depressed. It is a magnificent house and every sort of hygienic and proper arrangements were made, but oh the awful neatness and coldness and properness of the endless tiny beds with a chair by the side. Enormous dormitories with tiled walls and floors, oh so clean and so appallingly bare, huge windows, not even a blind, and the sisters who were gay charming and delightful, and who have only just been sent there, say the cold in winter is simply appalling. The children suffer terribly from cold, and till lately have had no hot water to wash in and no soap. It's all very stupid as just near is a huge boiler with endless hot water, which furnishes the great big laundry. The classrooms were better, but not a toy or a little chair or anything the least homey was there, and the tinies, who sang to us so well, were so terribly ugly, not one even fairly pretty, not even one that one would care to kiss. That I believe would be impossible in any country but Belgium, it is the ugliest race I've ever seen. We gave away a good deal of chocolate but one longed to give away hundreds of dolls and things, and break down some of the awful formality and dullness, and the frigidity of the whole place.

It is all wrong, kids ought not to be in institutions at all, and to see those terribly big rooms with the numbered beds, with the rooms where the little clothes were arranged so beautifully neatly in numbered shelves, it gave one a sort of nightmare. They ought to be boarded with fat comfortable in the country – and there are endless of these orphanages in this town. It is pitiable, tho' the sisters and the teachers all seemed very kind and nice. I was amused to see one woman with a sort of close blue cap and an overall in the Laundry, who was a sister and she had very sensibly taken off her horrid trappings for the work. I was told that if it had not been for the English who gave bones and scraps since the Armistice from the hospitals, these children would have starved. Flour here was 15 francs a pound the winter before last. Captain Harrison of the School of Cookery here has just told me they have practically no scraps, everything is used, and even during the advance and fighting, this Division sent home weekly enough dripping to make 500 tons of glycerine and owing [to] economy and arrangements made about men's rations, not drawing them when men were wounded or killed, they saved up such a supply that they were able to feed the refugees in Lille and other towns.

I only heard yesterday that our own dear friends where we buy buns, and where I pay over 2,000 francs a week, and who provide us, as gifts, with wonderful cakes – these people, who had worked frightfully hard, and got their own house and workshops in Rue St Nicolas and were very comfortably off, and spent any amount in charity, were driven out of their house at the point of a bayonet, and then had to stand and watch their place being looted and then fired and burnt to the ground. They lost everything, money, furniture, property, all. The street no longer exists, it is simply a pile of stone. They never mentioned this to me, I only heard of it from a friend who took them in for some time, until they started again from the very beginning and are now building up their business by degrees. I have never heard them say one word against the enemy.

Above left: Beatrice Gurney, Church Army. (MC 117/3)

Above right: Party for Belgian war orphans. (MC 117/3)

13 August 1919:

The children's party was a great success. Someone suggested flags and in one minute our garden, which has no flowers and is only a yard with cinders rolled as pavement, was gay with any number. Fred the head storesman, a delightful person who has 3 little girls and adores children, did most of the preparation and put up a long table for 40, which was made very gay with endless crackers found in the store, and heaps to eat, and before 4 the party arrived, 40 kids in black. Pinafores green and black, stiff Eton collars, and black and white washing hats. They looked so solemn, with 2 attendant sisters, one a charming and quite gay soeur superiere. The funny thing was they filed in 3 abreast and walked straight to the tea table and sat down. They never said how-do-you-do or looked our way. They were asked to tea and meant to have it. They were painfully silent at first and well behaved, and tried to stand up every time they were given food. We loaded the table with pistolets, buttered buns, open tarts, plums and cocoanut cakes, sent specially by the lady pattissier. They eat enormously and we had to get more and more supplies. The sister said they usually had ½ a tartine and café au lait, so she did not think she would give them any supper! They looked all fat and well and happy tho' the tragedy of their being in the orphanage was so terrible. Many were orphans of civilians shot by the Germans. Many no-one knew anything about at all. Children, babies found in the devastated areas, the youngest, a really darling little thing of about 4 was found as a tiny baby by its dead mother who had been killed by a bomb when fleeing from some ruined town. Many were ordinary war orphans. It was a good thing the sisters brought some small ones as they were very gay. However, the ice was broken when Richardson, our silent, shy, house orderly began to pull a cracker with one child, and then a delightful pandemonium began. They had never seen crackers and thought them sort of very smart 'serviettes', but they soon took to them and they looked really too gay for words all with coloured paper caps, simply bursting with joy. I hope the photographs will come off well. I was arm in arm with the pastry cook's wife surrounded by sisters (who adored being photographed) …

They laughed so we could not hear the piano and they took turns in pulling each other round and round in my little mitrailleuse cart, so soon to be taken to pieces to go with me to England – a use the Germans never thought of for it.

I could not buy them presents, except very few but looking at the vague bits of tape their pig tails were tied with, I asked the sister if the big ones would like hair ribbons. She simply roared with laughter. She was so tickled, and said it was the one thing they had une fievre about. That those very few who had a tiny bit of passable ribbon were the envied of them all, and the treasure was put in paper each Sunday to remain until the next great day. We promptly, Miss Gregory and I, went to our beloved bazaar and bought yards of it, and it was quite true, all control vanished and they became a fevered excited mob, quite well behaved but beside themselves with joy and fievre! We gave them little boxes of sweets before they left and got rid of them quite soon. They sang *God Save the King* awfully nicely, I had never heard it sung with French (or any other foreign words) before, and there were many more syllables than we have, which sounded so odd.

Famine in Russia

There were many starving children in Eastern Europe. The Society of Friends helped to alleviate the problems in Vienna along with other supporters, such as Ethel Williams, a Newcastle doctor born in Cromer, and Mabel Sheepshanks, daughter of the Bishop of Norwich. Norwich Quakers also took part in a mission to famine-ravaged parts of Russia.

Norwich Society of Friends' minutes for February 1922 record the following:

Contacts with great problems of world importance have been brought about through the call and response of Tom Copeman to work in famine-stricken Russia.

Tom Copeman's own diary survives:

In Buzuluk town and Ooyezd there were on May 1st of this year, 48 homes with 3,000 children which was about the normal number, but by October 1st there were 90 homes with 9,270 children — many of these homes emergency homes to accommodate children abandoned by their mothers. Yesterday we visited a six-roomed house which is being used as a receiving station for children picked up in the street, or even as sometimes happens left at our door by starving mothers. As a home it was intended for 50 children, but when our workers visited it on October 8th it had 364 and yesterday 654 children crammed within its walls.

Comments in a Quaker report include these:

The population is feeding mainly on substitutes. All the grass is eaten, and acorns and field rats are thought a luxury' … 'I saw in practically every house benches covered with birch or lime leaves. These are dried, pounded, mixed with acorns, some dirt and water, and then baked into a substance which they call bread, but which looks and smells like baked manure. The children cannot digest this food and they die.

Helping the afflicted carried its own risks: six of the first eighteen people to work with Tom Copeman in Russia caught typhus and one, Mary Patttison, died. She was followed to the grave by a second helper, Violet Tillard, who had been well known for her suffragette activities before the war, and who had helped found several suffragette groups in Norfolk. She was buried in Russia, and no less a figure than revolutionary leader Leon Trotsky reckoned her bravery to be as great as that of those soldiers killed in the war

The First World War was indeed total; women could die as bravely as men.

REFERENCES

All sources are held at the Norfolk Record Office, except as noted.

Text

Chapter 1:	MC 3126/1; SO36/25; MS 21382; D/ED 23/11; Norwich Girls' High School Magazine
Chapter 2:	ACC 2013/206; MC 643/16
Chapter 3:	UPC 188
Chapter 4:	MC 84/204, 205
Chapter 5:	MC 561/122, 123; Holt Post 22 June 1917; MC 4694/1; UPC 150
Chapter 6:	MC 947/1
Chapter 7:	MEA 11/112
Chapter 8:	*Carrow Works Magazine*
Chapter 9:	UPC 131; KIM9/18; MC 2969; MC 2175; MC 643/17; Holt Post 22 June 1917
Chapter 10:	GUN 187; Lestrange Supplementary 39a
Chapter 11:	MC 2847Q; *Carrow Works Magazine*
Chapter 12:	*Carrow Works Magazine*
Chapter 13:	Norwich Girls' High School Magazine; ACC 2014/28; C/ED 2 (school logbooks)
Chapter 14:	MC 117/3; SF 92; MS 10990